W9-CDW-573

WITHDRAWN
No longer the property of the
Boston Public Library.
Sale of this material benefits the Library

OMNIVM | LVX | CIVIVM

BOSTON
PUBLIC
LIBRARY

A HANDBOOK
for
EMERGENCIES

A HANDBOOK
for
EMERGENCIES

Coming Out Alive

by ANTHONY GREENBANK

Illustrated by Jerry Malone
and Mel Klapholz

DOUBLEDAY & COMPANY, INC.
GARDEN CITY, NEW YORK

LIBRARY OF CONGRESS CATALOGING IN PUBLICATION DATA
Greenbank, Anthony.
A Handbook for Emergencies
Published in 1975 under title:
Survival for Young People.
Includes index.
SUMMARY: A handbook of survival techniques
to be used in emergencies.
1. Accidents—Juvenile literature.
2. Survival (after airplane accidents, shipwrecks, etc.)—
Juvenile literature.   [1. Survival.   2. Accidents]
I. Malone, Jerry.   II. Title.
HV553.G73   1976   613.6′9
ISBN 0-385-09842-1 Prebound
ISBN 0-385-09822-7 Paperbound
Library of Congress Catalog Card Number: 74–25104

Copyright © 1975, 1976 by Anthony Greenbank
All Rights Reserved
Printed in the United States of America
First Edition

For Heather

CONTENTS

A HANDBOOK
for
EMERGENCIES

1

HOW TO USE
THIS BOOK

This book is about SURVIVAL—survival in situations
where average young people are confronted with unexpected
dangers. It does not tell you how to be a skilled climber, an
outstanding swimmer, or an exceptional athlete; indeed, such
people are just as likely as anyone else to succumb to a crisis
outside their own limited experience. Their very strength and
abilities may tempt them to take risks and make decisions
which a more prudent person would recognize as foolish.
Similarly, the best equipment can lure one into a false sense of
security, since equipment may be damaged or lost. What it
does tell you, however, is how to face danger and deal with it
in a rational way.

Most crises of survival occur out-of-doors and here we concentrate, therefore, on out-of-door situations, but many
alarming things can happen indoors (fires, mass panic, and so
on), and chapter 2 covers a number of such occasions. In all
these situations the crux of the matter is the same: How, by
careful preparation, can you avoid the panic actions that are
so often responsible for catastrophes when unexpected
dangers threaten your life? This book deals in detail with survival experiments which, if you practice them carefully,
should give you the confidence to face real emergencies with

the necessary coolness and take the kind of action necessary to get yourself out of a number of difficult situations.

These experiments will give you a knowledge you will never forget. They do, however, require guts and energy to complete —that is, if you carry them out properly. Never look on them as being anything but the REAL thing. Don't worry about the fact that you will be uncomfortable in these survival situations —even when you are only practicing them. Just concentrate on overcoming the problems as though your life depended on your actions. (One day it might.)

Start now. You can prove to yourself that you are more re-

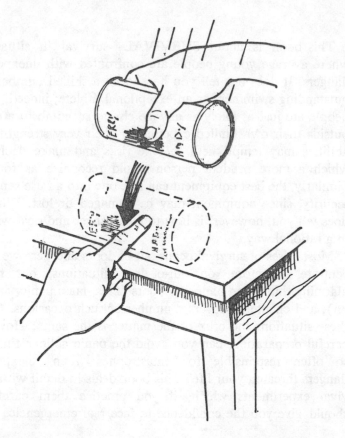

silient than you ever thought, and you need go no farther than the kitchen. Here is a survival experiment that will surprise you, and your friends.

Take a large size can of baked beans or some similar contents. An empty can is too easy for this experiment, so use only a full can, and one that has not been dented (as it certainly will be after this experiment!). Now, place the forefinger of your left hand—assuming that you are right-handed—on a strong, flat table top and press down. (Don't use a good table—it will suffer!) Hold the can in your right hand *with the seam of metal against your palm.* Take a deep breath and lift the can high above the finger. Then smash down the can, so that the center of the side of the can hits your finger. Do this with all your strength, as if to crush the finger. Only, that won't happen. Instead, your finger will feel nothing more than a mild blow, but the side of the can will be badly dented at the point where it hit your flesh and bone. If you wish to repeat the experiment, use a brand new can—and don't think that you can start gently and work up to a really hard hit. That way you would hurt yourself and, in any case, much of the value of the experiment would be lost.

Now, you see! You are tougher than you thought. The experiment, like many in this book, demands a certain amount of courage, but given the right advice you will come to no harm. And like many other experiments in the book it is not of direct value. It is unlikely that you will ever be called upon to bang your finger with a can of baked beans. It is also unlikely that you will suffer such extremes of hunger and thirst that you will need to eat a hedgehog or use a solar still to produce a small amount of water to drink. Softened as we are by civilization, tap water, television, telephones, the ubiquitous motorcar, and so on, make survival pretty easy for most people.

This, however, is the book for the sturdy individuals who want to feel independent of too many civilized aids; for who can tell what lies ahead for any one of us? And do we really want to reach a stage where a box of matches, a radio, tap water, electric light, and a motorcar are as indispensable to life as arms and legs? This book will, I hope, give you a new perspective against which to measure your place in the world (as well as give you a number of sound practical hints for use in everday life).

Every effort has been made to see that the instructions are clear and simple, but it is highly desirable that a young reader ask for the advice and approval of a responsible adult before embarking on any but the simplest experiments. BE CARE-FUL!

2

GETTING
TO THE STARTING POINT

LET'S start from—as the saying goes—Square One. Before you actually reach your mountain, forest, ocean, river rapids, or whatever wide-open spaces are the golden lure, you are going to have to get there just like any other expedition, whether it is bound for Patagonia or Alaska. Your transport, moreover, is likely to be bus or train rather than ship or plane . . . car or motorbike rather than a specially rigged, four-wheel-drive overland vehicle. Yet, as you are still heading into rough and adventurous countryside there is ample opportunity for all manner of things to go wrong—especially at this stage of your outdoor experience when you are pretty green. It is always a shame when you have your sights set on that distant adventure in the Great Outdoors, and then you are suddenly brought up with a jerk because the car you are traveling in gets stuck on a flooded road, your money is stolen, or your life is otherwise placed in danger through assorted emergencies which have nothing to do with outdoor survival; and your weekend or vacation is wrecked before it even started.

Accommodation for your trip, or part of that trip, will be new too. So you really need to be on your toes and know how to handle yourself whatever crises may arise. Often, these are the kind of situations which you laugh about afterward, but

they could develop into a nightmarish scene if you are caught
off guard when, say, your room catches fire.

Let us, then, split the chapter into two sections. The first
will deal with TRANSPORT emergencies—the kind of things
that go wrong while traveling to your chosen area of countryside and which could be perhaps from twenty to three
hundred miles from your home. The second section will cover
ACCOMMODATION survival: how to deal with accidents
when you reach the wilds and are living in a strange place. Incidentally, the following experiments in staying alive could be
useful whenever you travel.

TRAVEL SURVIVAL

Nothing much can go wrong on a bus, train, or car trip, or so
you might think. Do these tests and you will be surprised.
They will give you a good idea of some of the risks to come.

Young people are most vulnerable when carrying more
money than usual (as on long weekends and vacations). The
safest place for your funds is in a money belt worn beneath
your clothing. Stash most of the money inside here and carry
a small amount in a pocket for buying meals, tickets, or whatever else you need along the way. If you do not own a money
belt, carry your money distributed in the safest pockets for
securing coins and bank notes. You don't know which ones?
Well, try this.

Give a friend your wallet. Ask him to put it in a pocket of
his jeans. Tell him you will try to take it out without his no-
ticing in the next hour or so. You will find that if he put it in
the hip pocket, it is easy. But when it is placed in a front
pocket, it is next to impossible. Pickpockets find these front
pockets of pants the hardest of all to rob.

Repeat the experiment with your friend wearing a jacket—
the wallet goes into one of its pockets. Again, if the wallet is

slid into one of the side pockets, you will be able to slide it out again without the other person knowing. However, if he places it in the inside breast pocket, you will find it much more difficult.

The other safe place is inside your socks. Place the bank notes beneath the sole of your foot so that you can feel the money is there all the time and wherever you go.

HITCHHIKING SAFETY RULE

The simple rule is—DON'T. Police don't like you to beg lifts in any country. There are too many attacks and robberies when young people do this. However, there *are* times when you will need to. Your own transport breaks down, for example, and you need a lift to go for help. Or perhaps you are going to fetch help for someone who has had an accident and there is no other way you can travel.

Always take one precaution, though. When climbing into the car, jam your jacket sleeve in the door as you close it. Say, "Sorry, caught myself in the door. How do you open it?" Then reopen the door to free the material. This will show you which way to work the door handle. Remember, this can vary a great deal from car to car. Some doors have levers; others have buttons. There are push-toward-you handles and push-away knobs. Childproof locks may be in operation so that the handle you pull to open the door does not work until something else is pressed to release the lock, or, perhaps, the door can only be opened from the outside. Experiment from now on with all the cars in which you ride so that you become accustomed to the different door-opening devices. Make sure you know the difference between the door handle and the window winder, for example. And also that you know any locking button which has to be clicked free first before the door will open.

Then, knowing this, you can escape from a car all the more

easily if you have to. An example would be if you find yourself traveling with a recklessly fast driver. Say you are going
to be sick any moment, open the door as he stops, and get out
fast. DON'T get back in. Say you will walk to clear your
head. If you think you may be attacked or driven miles out of
your way, however, wait until the driver has to slow down and
stop—as at traffic lights on red. You will have a chance to
open the door and jump out.

STRONG-ARM TIPS

When you are young you can't hope to do much damage to an
assailant who is big and strong. He may even be knowledge-
able in the ways of judo, karate, Kung Fu, and wrestling, too.
Unlikely as it is that you are going to meet up with someone
who will try to grab you for some reason—and then harm you
—know that your best defense is to break his grip and run
like the wind. If it will help, shout.

Try the following ways to break holds. They hurt, and can
even injure people, so do not overdo it. But at least you will
learn that these very simple methods are effective when put to
the test. And after a lot of practice sessions you will be able to
do them instinctively.

Always avoid the offensive. Don't rush to fight back when
anyone grabs you. Go limp rather than resist. This puts your
attacker off his guard, and lets you have time to think what to
do next. This depends on what way he is grasping on to you.

Escape through the thumbs

When someone else has grabbed you by the wrists, the
weakest part of his grip is his thumbs. You can open them up
like a gate, letting your own arms escape. Here is how to do it.

If your practicing partner is holding your wrists tightly so
they are in front of your stomach, drop your hands a little
lower still. Then—suddenly—lift them high and outward . . .

Escaping through the thumbs

fast. If, instead, he is gripping your wrists so that they are in front of your face, do the opposite. Jerk them a bit higher, then swing them downward as hard as you can, spreading them wide apart at the same time. As long as you do either of these movements quickly and vigorously, you will be able to break a strong person's grip.

The same tactics will work, too, when you are held by one wrist in two fists. Bring your other hand between your protagonist's arms, and close it over your own fist, the one that is being grasped. Now, jerk both your arms upward or downward—depending on where the attacker is holding the wrist—and you will break the two-handed grip, too.

Pull the little finger

Try this with a pal. Let him hold you in a two-handed grip where you can't swing your arms because there isn't room. He will be forced to let go when you grab for one of his little fingers and bend it backward. It will break the grip he has on you most effectively. (Again, please be careful. Do it too vigorously and you could break the finger or put it out of joint.)

Step back quickly

If anybody grasps you from behind in any kind of hold, whether around your eyes, neck, chest, or waist . . . step back fast and stamp your heel down onto the instep of the person's foot which will be just behind you. If you miss the first time, bring it down again and keep repeating this kick until you can connect. An alternative is to bring your heel back hard into his shin.

Kick low down

An attack from a stronger person who is facing you can be staved off by turning your back on him, and kicking hard backward—like a pony or a horse—at his shin. Then, drag your shoe down his leg and tread on the top of his shoe. Do not practice this too violently with a friend, but get to know the movements.

If you try to kick high in front of you—like punting a football—it is easy for an attacker to grab your foot, causing you to fall flat on your back. Trying to kick with your knee can also be dangerous too since, again, the adversary can catch you around the knee, twist it, and send you spinning to the ground.

You can prevent someone from grabbing you around the throat very simply. Stretch out both arms in front of you and bend them up into the air from the elbows. Now cross the arms in front of your chin and neck so that the elbows are raised and your knuckles are pressing into the opposite armpits.

Defend yourself

If anyone ever comes at you with a bottle, club, stick, or even a knife . . . RUN. Keep as far away from him as possible. Jump over any handy fence, hedge, wall, table, or seat to put some distance between the two of you. Pad the lower part of one arm with a coat, jacket, or sweater to fend off any blows if the other person has you cornered. Sometimes you can grab something to use as a shield—a small table, thick branch, or anything of that sort, can absorb most of the blows. But do not make the mistake of trying to grab for the weapon with both your hands and wrestle it from the attacker.

USE YOUR BICYCLE FOR THESE TESTS

You can use a bicycle to simulate tricky driving, as when a motorist is suddenly faced with water over the road, thick mud resulting from a landslide, or snow and ice. It's handy to have the experience of keeping your wheels turning in such conditions, which can stop or seriously delay you. It is often the case that a motorist unfamiliar with such conditions can be helped through with advice from someone else who has had actual experience before of the same kind of conditions—you.

Try this in a shallow stream, pool, or pond at home, in preparation for when a cloudburst swamps a road you are traveling along. Ride your bicycle through the shallowest part without getting your feet wet. If you do get wet shoes, consider it the same as a motorist going in too deep and too fast so that water drenches the distributor and gets sucked up the exhaust pipe (both of which will stop a car).

First, you must check to be sure the water isn't too deep.

Wade through, looking for the route which will take your bike across without water coming over the top of the chain. Plot this route by pushing sticks or branches into the water as signposts. Then, ride through slowly, following this route. If you were driving a car, you would slip the clutch so as to keep your speed down, yet still maintain fairly high revs—to keep backwater from coming up the exhaust (and also to stop it from splashing over the distributor which happens if you crash into water at full speed).

Select the lowest gear on your bike. Stand on the pedals and prod them down in quarter-way jerks (or less) to ease your way forward. The foot pressing the pedal down only does this for about ten inches, then you can bring this pedal back up a few inches before tapping it down again—as if you are competing in a slow bike race.

Use the same pedal to power you through, only turning the pedal crank full circle when you feel you are traveling so slowly you will fall. Balance any wobble by adjusting your body weight on both pedals like a motorbike-trials rider and turning the front wheel sharply in the direction of any possible fall. Then, once the wobble is corrected, turn it back again.

If your feet get only slightly damp, your car will probably get through. Wet ankles and shoes, though, mean a car driven the same way as you rode would have stalled in the water. There is one last important thing to do—dry out the brakes of your bike before taking to the road again (by riding with the brakes partly on).

Drench a grassy slope with buckets of water, for example. Again, you will soon discover the only way to cycle across it is by the slow bicycle race principle. Keep stopping the pedals down, relax the pressure, and then press on a pedal again. Turn the front wheel this way and that, adjusting your balance as you stand on the pedals, progressing in small jerks. However, select your highest, or next to the highest, gear for mud. Too low a gear encourages wheelspin, and you get bogged down.

The same principles hold with a car. The driver should be in second or third gear, handling the revs carefully to avoid unnecessary wheelslip, and he should be ready to go into reverse if there is any sign of the car sticking fast. If he does become stuck, then the car may have to be jacked up so that stones, foliage, sacks, or any other material that will give the wheels a grip can be placed under the tires.

Ride a bike in snow with flat tires, and then with the tires normally inflated. Which gives better road grip? Most people think to let the air out is easier, but it is not. It also damages the tire. Have your bike tires at the usual pressure instead and try the slow bicycle race system on snow-clad or icy roads. Go very carefully. But don't use the lowest gear. Ease your bike delicately forward with a nudge on the pedal here and a slightly sharper jab on it there. You will find it helps to pack heavy stones in the saddlebag—this works with cars too. They should carry any weight available as ballast over the driving wheels. Only apply the brakes very gently and when you are traveling in a straight line. Don't suddenly strain them, though. Use a pumping action on the brake to avoid skidding. A car should be driven on snow and ice according to these principles, too. If it becomes stuck in deep ruts, however, advise the driver not to rev in an effort to speed out fast. Try reversing, then going forward, then reversing again with a gentle burst of the throttle, thus setting up a rocking motion which can then allow the car to be driven on slowly. Still no use? Then you will have to dig ruts below and in front of the wheels. When these grooves are packed with stones, car floor mats, and anything else handy, the car can be driven out over them . . . as long as the wheels are pointing in a straight line with the rest of the car. If the wheels are pointing at an angle, it can prove next to impossible to shift the vehicle.

ARRIVAL POINT SURVIVAL

You have reached the log cabin, youth hostel, chalet, caravan, mobile home, barn, shack, shed, mountain refuge, old quarry hut, or hotel in sight of the hills, within earshot of the rapids, shaded by pines, and fanned with the breeze. But, whatever it is, there are certain risks you must now look out for. They are present in all kinds of buildings—yes, including your home. In fact, you can now try the following experiments *at* home so that you are ready for any eventuality.

FIRE FIGHTING

If lighting a fire is one of the most important aspects of survival in the wilderness—and, as we shall see, it is—then extinguishing fires can prove even more vital, especially now, when a fire in a building can get out of control. You will probably be a long way from any Fire Station, so you need to know what to do if there is any chance of your having to put a fire out.

Light a series of small bonfires on open ground, throw a little paraffin on them *from a safe distance* so that they flare. Then douse the flames as quickly as possible.

Imagine the fire is inside a room. Your first action should be to shut all doors and windows to prevent air currents from fanning the fire. You can see the effect of this measure now. Place boards, planks, large pieces of wood, or any other not obviously inflammable material immediately around the fire. The flames will soon die down, although they will take time to go out; you can now hit them more easily with other fire-fighting tactics.

Throw water over a bonfire. You will kill it at once, as long as there is plenty of water. However, there are two exceptions [in a building when water must NOT be used.] One is when the water could hit live electric wires, in which case a shock could speed back and electrocute you. The other is when a pan of fat or oil is burning. Throw water on the flames and you will scatter them all around the room since burning oil floats on water. These tips will help:

> Use whatever is handy for carrying the water —buckets, climber's hardhats, boots, rucksacks, even canoes.

> The person throwing the water on the fire should get as near to the flames as possible by holding some sort of shield in front of him (a wet garment, small table, chair, etc). This way the water can be thrown straight into the middle of the flames.

> Form a chain of helpers to pass the water from the nearest supply, whether it is a tap or a stream.

Do remember, though, if the fire is in a building, before throwing any water, switch off the electricity supply at the fuse box and at any appliance which may be on fire (like a TV). You can always pull out the plug first.

Build a small bonfire in an old frying pan. The flames would look nasty in a kitchen, yet they are easily checked. Throw a damp cloth or pan lid over the flames. Press down and smother the flames.

A larger bonfire burning on the ground can be extinguished the same way, but it should not be too hot. (If so, water is the safest method.) Shovel sand, soil, or dirt on the flames and watch them die. A wet cloth (or even a dry one will work) can also be used to snuff out the flames. Try pressing the fabric down with a long branch or by stamping on the edges. This helps put out the fire even quicker.

Burning clothes

DO NOT TRY THIS. Imagine it instead. If a friend's clothes have caught fire, knock him down to the ground with a shoulder charge. Roll him in the nearest piece of carpet, rug, mat, curtains, or garment. When there is nothing handy, fling yourself on top and smother the flames this way. Of course, it may be YOU who is on fire. Still carry out the same action. Throw yourself on the ground and roll over and over, preferably wrapping something around you. The danger when you keep standing is that flames can run up past your face.

Trapped by fire

The first experiment here is important. All too often people have been trapped inside a sleeping bag because they did not know how to get out of it quickly when their room was on fire. Fail to wriggle out of a nonzip sleeping bag in time, and flames will get you. Practice a quick exit.

Climb in and out of your sleeping bag by pulling it on and off like a sock. Sit on the floor, pull the bag up to your thighs until your toes are pressing against the end of the bag. Now lie down and draw it up to your chest in one movement.

To get out fast . . . do the same in reverse. Sit up, pull the bag down to your waist, lie back down, lift your hips, and push the bag down over your legs in one go.

Imagine waking up in the night and smelling smoke. Do you know which is the best escape route when your building is on fire? Would you know what you should do when the doorknob scorches your hand as you grab for it? These, and other questions, can be answered best if you keep thinking about them wherever you are. First, always think of Edith: that is, Exit Drill in the Home.

Jot down now the different ways of escape from your bedroom at home. There should be at least one second way out from the hall—perhaps through another bedroom (if flames are coming up the stairs) and out through the window to drop onto the roof of a low shed underneath. In large buildings like hostels and hotels there is something wrong if such an emergency way out is not obviously marked with arrows and clear directions. If not—ask why. There must be an alternative route, and *you* should be the one to find it. (So many of us simply do not bother.) Now, suppose you have already checked out the fire escape route but cannot reach it? What now? It is too late; the flames are right outside the door and . . . Well, do this next experiment.

Imagine that you wake up and smell something burning in the night, run to open the door and the doorknob is too hot to handle. This means the fire is right outside and you are trapped. If you were to open the door by padding the doorknob with a cloth and twisting, fumes and flames would be sucked into the room. . . . So, really try to picture this scene and *mentally* go through the following actions in your bedroom.

DO NOT OPEN THE DOOR. It will have to burn down first before the flames can reach you. This could with luck take the better part of an hour.

TRY TO ESCAPE THROUGH A GROUND-FLOOR WINDOW. Throw a chair through it in a crisis if there is no other way and you are certain of getting out. (Remember about the peril of drafts which come through open windows.)

WHEN YOU ARE TOO HIGH FROM THE GROUND, SEAL THE BOTTOM OF THE DOOR WITH A CARPET OR RUG. This will help to keep out smoke and fumes.

KEEP YOUR HEAD NEAR THE FLOOR IN THICK SMOKE. The air is clearer near the floor. After calling and waving for HELP at the open window, wait until help arrives. A wet hanky in front of the mouth and nose helps to prevent coughing; however, it doesn't stop dangerous fumes.

WHEN THERE IS NO CHANCE OF HELP FROM OUTSIDE—AND THE DOOR IS BURNING DOWN —GET READY FOR THE LAST RESORT. Make a rope by tearing sheets, blankets, and curtains and knotting them. (Use square knots.) Tie one end to the heaviest piece of furniture you can find. Then lower yourself out of the window and slide down, hand over hand. This is not easy, and it should be left until everything else has failed. The worst thing of all you can do, though, is jump from a height. Even jumping from a very modest height can break a limb, and possibly kill.

Fire-flight jump

Practice this from a low window or tree so that, when hanging by your fingertips from a sill or a branch, your feet are your own height from the ground. Let go and hit the ground, bending your legs to take the shock. Then, try it by taking off from a sitting position on the window sill or tree branch. You will not want to jump now. The reason is that hanging from your hands reduces the actual distance you have to jump by a good few feet or so (and more if you're tall). This is quite a long way—enough to make the difference between a bad landing, simply hitting the ground hard, and a sprained ankle.

As we have already seen, the best way out of a burning house could be through a window. Such a jump, say, from a first-floor window, may be the only way to safety. And to do it with any degree of safety you must hang from your hands before taking the plunge.

Survival jump from first-floor window, preferably onto shed roof below—or other soft landing

GAS AND ELECTRICITY

If you smell gas, act fast. First, open all the windows. Then, check the building to see that all the gas taps are turned off. Turn the gas off at the main, and call the gas company. (The gas main's tap will probably be near the gas meter.) NEVER look for a leak with a naked flame.

The gas will smell most strongly when you are near the leak. Another way of tracing the leak is to wipe soapy water along the pipes and joints—escaping gas will show by blowing bubbles. You can make an emergency repair by painting over the leak, wrapping a strip of cloth around it while the paint is still wet, then cover everything in insulating tape. If the smell of gas disappears, you should be able to use the gas if you *have* to. But you should still report the leak. Natural gas, as opposed to coal gas, is nonpoisonous, but just as explosive!

Check the fuses when several lights go out. First, switch off the current at the fuse box. Make sure there is not more than one fuse box; there may be two or three such switches. Test lights and electric appliances in different rooms to make sure you have killed the current, then open up the fuse box. Take out each fuse in turn and see if the fuse wire stretched between two terminals has melted.

Sometimes the wire runs through a hole. Test this with the point of a penknife blade. The fuse wire is broken if you can pull one end loose.

Use proper fuse wire to replace the wire. If you use wire that is too thin, the fuse will soon burn out. Too thick a wire, though, means overheating, causing a potential fire risk.

Today's wiring systems have fused plug sockets. Each plug has its own fuse shaped like a small capsule. If an electric wire fails, therefore, open up the plug and replace the fuse with one of the correct wattage. You need a 3-amp cartridge fuse for up to 700 watts, a 7-amp fuse for up to 1,500 watts, or a 13-amp fuse for up to 3,000 watts.

INTRUDERS

NEVER try to grab a burglar or prowler yourself. Telephone the police, or get help, if this seems the only way at the time.

If you arrive back at your home from home in the wilds, and you think someone is inside who should not be there—do not rush inside. Make plenty of noise outside, however, and this will give whoever it is the chance to leave the building.

(Burglars will usually leave themselves an escape route, and it is better they use this than attack you.)

Keep quiet if you wake in the night to find someone else in your room. Pretend to be sound asleep. And do not snatch up a weapon if you hear noises from somewhere else. It could be wrenched from you and used against you.

Always lock doors and windows in all parts of the building. Slide bolts into place; keep doors on chains provided. Never leave keys on the inside of doors. (A burglar puts a sheet of paper under the door, pushes out the key from the outside with a piece of wire, the key then falls on top of the paper which the burglar then slides under the door. He now has the key in his hand ready for use.)

Place a chair with its back resting against the door of your bedroom so that it leans up under the doorknob. Ask a friend to try to push the door open from the outside. You will then be able to work out the best angle to tilt the chair, and how to stop the chair legs from slipping. Place a rug, rubber mat, or anything made from leather under these. Another way is to stick them in your climbing boots so the chair legs force the rubber soles onto the floor. You can use this effective improvised lock to make sure *your* room door is well secured wherever you are. And if you are ever in a perilous position, where the door is being charged and battered by someone from the other side, then reinforce any bolts, locks, or chains *with the chair method—outlined above—as well.* The reason is that bolts, locks, and chains may look secure, but they are only as strong as the screws holding them—and these may be puny.

3

HOW TO MAKE
TWO SURVIVAL KITS

The combat pilot's *final* survival hope is not his parachute nor is the shipwrecked sailor's last-ditch savior his rubber dinghy. Both parachute and dinghy are simply the means of leaving a stricken plane or boat and staying alive *for the moment.*

Then, if the survivors are still not located by rescuers, they have one last hope: the survival kit. Such a package will contain vital supplies to give them a fighting chance wherever they happen to end up—perhaps a desert island, the jungle, or on the top of an iceberg.

During World War II, aircrews of some nationalities carried their survival kits disguised as personal possessions. A chain saw was concealed in the lacing of their boots—it was capable of cutting through iron bars. An ordinary fountain pen contained ink, pep pills, a compass, a colored map of Europe on crumple-proof rice paper, and two sachets of dye so that a uniform could be dyed a different color and look like civilian clothing. Magnetized lengths of metal were also slid into pencils so that when they were hung from a thread they always swiveled north. And some uniforms had buttons which were magnetic—you tore off such a button, mounted it on to another, and the magnetic button then turned to point north.

Even heavy flying boots had extra uses. The warm woolly

parts could be ripped off and transformed into a cozy jacket —by the use of press studs. Yet enough remained of the boots themselves to form a sturdy pair of walking shoes.

So it should be with you—always carry emergency supplies whether you plan to paddle a canoe, pedal a bicycle, hike a mountain, float a dinghy out to sea, scale a rock face by the roadside, or take part in any other adventurous pursuit outdoors.

Survival supplies take up very little room in your pocket, rucksack, boat, or whatever, and you can have a great deal of fun assembling two survival kits at home today for the price of a pack of cigarettes. One is for your rucksack, one for your pocket.

The survival kit for your pocket should be carried *everywhere*. It is designed to fit into your pocket and as such you are never without it; it fits into a fountain pen.

The survival kit for your rucksack is the one you hope you have with you, however. It is contained in a small tin can with a firmly fitting lid. But, should your rucksack be lost, spilled, damaged, or otherwise unobtainable, then you will have to rely on the fountain pen survival kit. It may not be much, but it is something to fall back on. Always remember, carrying both survival kits helps in various ways. By knowing you are reinforced with supplies for lighting a fire, for example, they can be a source of strength when you are swimming in ice cold water over the last few yards to the shore and you feel your strength fading. You *know* there is still hope as long as you keep struggling on.

Survival kits will also back you up on the various simulated but nevertheless true-to-life survival experiments in this book. When all else has failed, and you are paying the penalty for being careless or unlucky, the survival kits will give you a last chance. Most important, however, is the fact that they will always help you in an emergency.

Needless to say, you should practice thoroughly first with

each of the two survival kits at home. Their contents may seem sparse, but they ARE most effective when used properly, and you will be able to get the best out of them by trying the survival kit experiments given in this chapter until you are practice perfect.

The best way is to make up the two kits at home and seal them with tape to make them waterproof. Then set about practicing the experiments to come with contents similar to those you packed, *and those contents only*.

For example, if you set out to light a bonfire using only the ingredients contained in the fountain pen survival kit, and fail, then you must consider yourself as being in great danger (although you are only simulating the tragedy). It is no use continuing to try to ignite the twigs with extra matches and minicandles. Instead, you must scrap that effort and begin again from scratch with new fire-lighting materials and a new allocation of survival kit supplies. This way you can see if you improve this time, and then—as you become more proficient —you will also be able to cut down on the number of matches used too. This means that out of the smallest number of fire-lighting ingredients, you would still be able to start several fires in a real-life accident.

Always carry the sealed survival kits with you when venturing outdoors.

TIN CAN SURVIVAL KIT

The contents will give you SHELTER, WARMTH, FOOD, and SOS SIGNALS. They are a final escape hatch that would keep you alive in a real emergency. It will take some thought and a little patience to make this survival kit, because you have to squash everything into as small a space as possible. However, although it may seem a difficult job to push everything into such a small space, you will be doubly glad should you ever need them in an emergency. So keep at it.

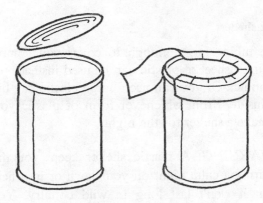

Tin can survival kit

Look for a suitable empty can at home. Wash it out and dry thoroughly. There is no special can that is best, just the smallest you can find that will still hold the contents listed below. For example, you can buy a survival kit the size of a small paperback. Your kit could well be smaller and weigh less. After all, survival suits for sailors, comprising of boots, down-lined pants, coat, hood, and gloves, fit into a space only the size of a large thermos bottle. Select a can that you will be able to use as a small cooking pot, too. When you have packed everything inside, seal the lid down with bright glo-colored tape. However, be careful not to overdo this. There have been occasions when survivors have succumbed in the end because they were too weak to undo the too-well secured lid of their survival kits. You may find it easier to choose your can, incidentally, after first gathering the following items—and doing the suggested survival experiments as you go along.

BODY SHELTER

Quickly available body shelter is important. You need to stay dry and stop the wind from stealing your body's heat. Lack of shelter is a major factor in death from hypothermia.

Plastic shelters

Polythene tubing large enough to cover you comfortably is ideal. A single sheet of plastic can be used instead, provided it is large enough. Or you can use a large plastic bag big enough to squat inside. From whichever form of plastic you choose, you can make a shelter for the night.

> WARNING: A plastic shelter keeps you dry during a calm night on your lawn or in a field but it won't last long in wild country. You must always build a windbreak to save it from strong breezes, or construct it in front of a large boulder or wall, for example. Only then are you safe—the plastic keeping you dry and cocooning you in an envelope of warm air. Plastic shelters are better than nothing, but you will need to practice with them before it is safe to use them.

Let's look more closely at the three different types of plastic —*the tube, the sheet,* and *the bag*—and the kinds of shelters we can construct as a result. Then choose the kind of plastic you prefer. You can try shelters developed from all three sources on any plot of grass near home.

The bivvy bag

"Bivvy" stands for bivouac, which is something you must do when caught out in rough country at nightfall. A proven piece of emergency equipment with mountaineers, the idea of the bivvy bag is simple. You sit inside it. And this large bag which can be made from the same kind of material as kitchen plastic wrapping will keep you warm. As long as you leave the hole at the top open and in front of your face (enabling you

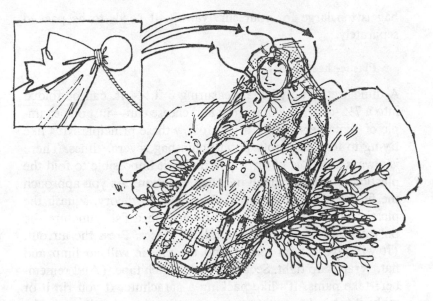

Bivvy bag

to breathe) the plastic will cocoon warm air around you. If possible, sit on something other than the cold ground—such as a pile of branches and leaves. And stick your feet inside your rucksack, drawing this as high up your legs as it will go. Be careful not to rip the plastic. Quite thin gauges of ordinary plastic will provide warmth, but they also tear more easily. Usually bivvy bags are made from thick plastic. Although a drawstring around the mouth of the bag is ideal, you won't be able to manage one with an ordinary big plastic bag. However, you can knot part of the opening together as shown in the illustration. Tie a small round pebble at three or four separate points into the edge of the plastic with a length of string. This now means you have three or four pieces of string attached to the plastic, and they form a type of drawstring with which to knot up the bag once you are inside it. Don't tie the strings too tightly, though. Note: Because of its size, a bivvy bag is too large for your survival kit. It needs to be packed separately.

Plastic-sheet shelters

A thin sheet of polythene measuring 6 ft.×4 ft. can be folded into a 7½-oz. Heinz macaroni and cheese can—just one example of container—easily if you follow these principles. It's like trying to fold an empty potato chip bag several times. There is always a bubble of air which makes it impossible to fold the plastic into a really small package. Solution? As you approach the final folding-over stages which will, in theory, squash the plastic into a pack which can be held in a fist, puncture the polythene with a pin in a couple of places. Press the air out. (It will give a faint hiss.) And the plastic will go limp and flat. Wrap it up tight. Secure it with Scotch tape. (And remember: take pains. It's like packing a parachute. If you rip it or make it too bulky so that you cannot get the other items in the tin can, you might as well forget it.)

You can make two kinds of emergency tents from a single sheet of plastic. The first type is the lean-to; the second, the ridge tent-shaped bivvy. Both use the same principles of construction which are based on lots of string and the use of heavy stones as anchors. It's just their shapes that differ.

Let's look at the lean-to first. You attach the top edge of the sheet to a wall or large boulder with string as shown in the diagram. And then you pin the bottom edge of the plastic to the ground with heavy rocks tied to the sheet with string. Then beneath the 45° slope of the roof you have your shelter. Exactly how you arrange your plastic sheet each time depends on the layout of the terrain and the type and position of the supporting wall, boulder, hedge, fence, or whatever. But certain rules should always be followed.

Tie string around small pebbles to the plastic at each corner and also at one-foot intervals along the edges of the sheet. Leave the string in place when you pack the plastic sheet into the survival kit.

Use HEAVY rocks for the anchorage on the ground. Stones that are too light will slide over the grass and slacken the roof of your shelter. You need a big rock for each corner, then one for each length of string already tied in place in between.

Make sure your shelter sheet is as taut as a clenched fist. Slack plastic sheets let in rain and are more vulnerable to the wind.

The top edges of the sheet must be tied securely. But check that the anchoring points are safe. Don't tie the sheet strings to stones on the top of a wall which are unstable and which could drop on you in the night. A good method is to push strong twigs into chinks in the wall and tie your sheet to these.

Pad between rocks and plastic with moss, grass, ferns, or anything else which helps prevent the sheet rubbing through.

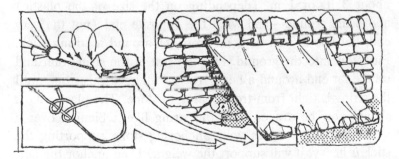

Lean-to bivouac

The ridge tent-shaped plastic-sheet shelter is just as easy to make. In fact, this shelter can be made in places where there are no walls, no fences, no hedges, and no boulders. It can be built between two piles of stones, or between a tree and a pile of stones, or between a rucksack standing on the ground and a piece of stick. There is no end to the variations you can use. The diagram shows the principle, and now it's up to you.

A-shaped bivouac

Tie, for example, one end of a long length of string (about 12 ft. or 4 m., say) around a tree, fence post, or boulder— about 3 ft. or 1 m. (depending on the size of the plastic) above the ground—and wind the opposite end (not the very end, but about 3 ft. or 1 m. from it) around a strong stick. Push this into the ground. Pull the rest of the string taut and tie the far end around a heavy rock. Pull back this stone until the string is tight from tree to stick to stone. The plastic sheet should now be draped over the string like a blanket over a clothesline. As long as your anchoring stone supporting the stick *is* heavy, it will support the weight. Then anchor the bottom edges of the A-shaped tent with heavy stones—just as you did with the lean-to design. Square up the shelter by sliding the stones until the plastic is as straight and tight as glass.

Tube tent

You need strong horticultural plastic tubing about 6 ft. (2 m.) long and 4 ft. or 5 ft. (1.5 m.) across when stretched out on the ground. Strangle one end of the tube in a fist and knot this with a length of string which you leave tied on. Then attach three pieces of string to the other mouth of the tube using the pebble method of knotting string to plastic. The three pebbles should be spaced at equal intervals, and although two of the pieces of string need be only a couple of feet long each, the third piece—it doesn't matter which—should be around 10 ft. (3 m.) long.

To pitch the tube tent, flatten it out on the ground. You will need four heavy stones, one of which is tied to the string at the strangled end of the tube. Twist the tube around until the two shorter pieces of string at the mouth of the tent are lying on the ground. Knot these to heavy rocks too. Pull them outward so that between the three rocks already tied to the tube the floor of the tent is roughed out. This leaves the long string until last. As shown in the drawing, this is now twisted around the top of a strong stick standing a few inches away from the mouth of the tent and jabbed firmly in the ground—just as in the A-shaped plastic-sheet tent detailed above. The strong stick jacks up the opening of the tube tent into an A shape too, and then the long string—after being hitched to near the top of the stick—is anchored to a fourth heavy rock. All four rocks are readjusted until the tube is standing as a wedge-shaped structure: solid, taut, and ready to sleep in.

There is one more experiment to try at this stage: spend a night near home in one of the plastic tents. This will enable you to get the feel of spending a night under something so thin you can actually see the stars. It gives you the experience of mild survival. And such practice is absolutely vital.

Keep everything simple—just your plastic shelter and a

sleeping bag (or a few blankets wrapped around you). You should choose a warm evening, anyway, so that you will be comfortable. And it is best to be close to home so that if things do go wrong, you haven't far to go for help.

The golden rules are: pitch the door of your shelter away from the wind; ensure your shelter is behind some form of windbreak, whether a wall, hedge, or building; lie directly on the ground only if you want to find out how cold it becomes, otherwise make a mattress on the floor of your shelter with anything appropriate to a survival situation: newspapers, foliage, and so on; try not—although it will be difficult—to press up against the walls of your shelter (however, there should be little condensation if you leave a gap at the opening of the shelter); block off some of the opening end or doorway to your tent with stones, a rucksack, boughs, anything available; keep a flashlight by you in case you need to readjust things in the night; make a pillow from a sweater or some other garment resting on a pile of ferns, grass, bracken, or leaves.

An alternative to a plastic bag or plastic sheet is the space rescue blanket—a compact piece of emergency equipment worth knowing about, although it is not as versatile as a big plastic bag. It is a blanket made of plastic film coated with aluminum—a typical size is 56 in.×84 in. (1.30 m.×2 m.). It is windproof and waterproof and reflects back 90 per cent of the body's natural heat. One side is orange for visibility against snow, the other silver to reflect heat. It weighs no more than a small apple, folds to the size of a cigarette pack, and can be carried in your pocket (or a large survival kit tin can container). It is quite cheap and can be bought from camping supply shops. Plastic sheet, though, is more versatile and generally stronger.

WARMTH

Inner and outer body warmth are provided by the fire you will be able to light. It then melts snow, heats water, dries wet clothing, cheers you up, and helps attract searchers. Your metal cooking pot—the tin can container of your survival kit—can be used to brew tea that warms you inside, while the fire's warmth removes the chill outside.

Matches

Store your matches of the nonsafety type inside your survival kit can. Wooden ones are best. Make them up into a "raft" in

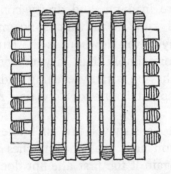

Match raft

the following way. Dip the heads of about twenty matches into hot candle wax. Let the wax grow cold so that the heads are then waterproofed. Now lay ten matches together on the top of greaseproof paper. Arrange them so that they lay next to each other, and so that the heads are placed at alternate ends. One head is at the top of the row, the head of the next match is at the other end, the head of the third match is at the top of the row again, and so on. This ensures that no heads touch and therefore accidentally detonate each other by rubbing together. Drip hot candle wax over the matches and while it is still warm press the remaining ten matches close together across them—the heads again alternating so they don't touch each other. The two layers of matches now make a two-layered raft which is glued together with the candle wax once it goes cold. The matches will still light should they ever be dropped into water. And they float. (Pack with matchbox striking paper.)

Survival experiments in lighting bonfires are very important. Canadian and Alaskan bush pilots, for example, light a fire immediately after an emergency landing in the wilderness, they rate it such a vital matter. Now, it is practically impossible to light a fire in damp and drafty conditions without a number of trial runs in advance—no matter how many matches you may have. Nowhere is the struggle for survival demonstrated more simply than in your trying to light a fire with a few matches on a rainy evening and ending up struggling as you desperately try to blow tiny red embers into a blaze.

Setting light to a survival fire isn't like igniting a camp bonfire, where you have fuel and matches at hand, and you can always try again if the first attempt doesn't succeed. *This could be your one and only chance.*

Nature's fire lighter is birch bark. Dip birch bark into water, and light it with a match at one corner. The wet strip will burst into flames. So, peel away thin onionlike layers of this bark and keep them in one of your pockets. Incidentally, as with all the other fire-lighting materials you have to find first before you light your fire—collect plenty. You can never collect too large an amount of burnable items, especially highly inflammable ones like birch bark. Now look for more *tinder.*

Fill a pocket with anything dry that can be ground to

powder—crumbling wood, pocket fluff, pine needles, lichen, dead ferns, bat droppings, old moss, dried grass, down from birds' nests, shirt/sweater/cardigan threads, wisps of sheep's fleece, and anything else at all which can be reduced to tiny fragments between thumb and forefinger, or which can be torn into confettilike paper like pencil sharpener shavings.

If your clothing is wet and all your pockets are damp, then two big slabs of bark that are dry on one side can protect your fire until it is ready. Lay your tinder on one dry piece of bark on the fire site, then place the other piece over it until you have collected all your firewood. The next step is *kindling*.

Look farther afield now for anything burnable that is still small—paper rolled into balls, splinters of wood, pieces of bark, pine cones, wood shavings, feathers, twigs. Go for dry, brittle wood which snaps easily. Really dry wood, moreover, doesn't have any bark. If wood feels cold and heavy, it is probably damp and won't burn easily. Look for kindling beneath thick foliage and shrubs, especially when it's raining. You can also snap dead branches from trees. Forget about branches bearing leaves, however, because they will burn slowly and only be of use once the fire is burning well. One more hint, too, about collecting kindling: you can always cut into damp, dead wood with a knife or batter it to bits with a rock and obtain dry kindling from the wood inside.

Scour around for larger pieces of fuel and make a really big stockpile of fuel for your fire once it is burning. Damp wood can be collected now, but you will need to dry it out first by the flames before feeding it into them. Look for softwoods like spruce, fir, hazel, and pine, rather than hardwoods like oak, beech, poplar, and birch. However, once the fire is roaring well, you can throw any kind of wood onto it. And, although split branches burn better than whole ones, you must be prepared to use whole tree limbs once the flames have gained a hold, if you find it impossible to break down the branches in

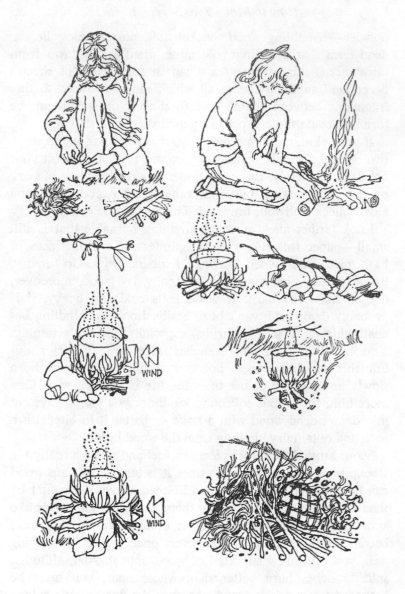

Lighting fires and boiling water

any other way. Finally, it is most important that you have all your wood and kindling on hand before you strike a match. And plenty of it.

The first thing to keep in mind when lighting a survival fire is not to make it too big. Small fires are easier to control; they use less fuel and their heat can be concentrated (the exception being, of course, when you are signaling for help and need a big display of flames). Scrape away a large circle of ground clear of vegetation—especially in woodland—so that flying sparks cannot set fire to trees and undergrowth. The next step is to make a platform in the middle of your clearing for the fire. This can either be made from logs laid across each other, one layer going one way, the layer above going the other, or you could build the fire on flat stones. However, it pays to experiment with building fires on snow too, since you will need an extra large platform of green wood here, otherwise your fire will fall through any depth of snow and disappear. Select a sheltered area out of the wind, if at all possible, where the fire won't spread, and again have all the kindling and larger lumps of fuel at hand ready for when you first light the tinder.

The tinder should then be taken from your pocket and carefully stacked in a small heap with the most powdery and shortest bits of dried material at its base. Around this can then be built a larger pyramid of kindling. Don't pack too many pieces on this layer and avoid letting it crowd the tinder. As long as the flames from the tinder can touch the kindling that's fine. To ignite the tinder; place a small piece of candle with the wick exposed beneath the tinder pile—you can do this through the opening you left in the kindling. Light the candle, remembering to replace your matches at once in a dry place. Keep in mind that it is by far the best idea to begin with a small fire and add to it as the blaze grows.

Now, certain things will help your fire burn more quickly if you do them from the beginning. For example, you should take strips of the finest birch bark, which we mentioned earlier, and thread this in strands through the tinder and then, in larger pieces, through the kindling. Leave plenty of spaces in the kindling so that the draft can blow through without hindrance. Blowing gently on the burning wood helps to increase the flames. When you do add the heavier fuel, once the kindling is in the grip of good flames, do so piece by piece. If you squash the kindling with too heavy a fuel at first, you'll put the fire out. Instead, make a point of not putting too many pieces of wood on the flames, nor chunks of fuel that are too heavy so they weigh the rest down. As the fire grows then you can nudge in the ends of logs arranged like the spokes of a wheel around the hub—the hub being the actual fire itself. Gradually push each log in as the end of each log becomes more and more charred.

Keep the firewood that is still in waiting dry under cover. Dry any wood that is damp by the fireside. This goes especially for kindling which you should use for the next fire. Keep plenty in stock. But still it's better that you keep fires going overnight than to keep relighting them (using up matches, tinder, and kindling in the process). To do this, a heap of ashes over the embers works. You scrape them away next morning, and the coals will still be glowing beneath. Or you can lay two or three logs over the flames. The idea is that the fire really scorches these, and *then* you lay a thin layer of dry earth and ashes. In fact, this last method is the best.

Candle

Trim a candle with a knife until it fits comfortably into your survival kit—not that paring is usually necessary. It will be of more use for lighting fires than as an end to seeing in the dark generally speaking. However, it has other uses too. It will help light S.O.S. flares from rags, etc., fast. It will act as a miniature cooker—though only for a short period—if you place it upright in the bottom of the survival kit can, having punched holes in the sides of this container for draft, and place a cooking receptacle such as a paper pan for boiling water on top. And it will provide food where conditions are permanently warm but where you are short of food—desperately short, that is. Know your candles, however, for most candles today are made from paraffin wax which consist of hydrocarbons with no food value other than psychological. Tallow candles made from beef or hog fat are best for eating.

Fuzzsticks

Take a straight-grained stick—preferably of softwood—and cut one end into a mass of curls with a number of single knife strokes. Three such fuzzsticks are enough to start a fire when the curly ends are placed together and lit; they are a type of Nature's candle. So, when you have used up the candle in the survival kit in a real survival situation, replace it with a couple of twiglet shaved fuzzsticks or three of them—if you have room.

Charred cloth

Not mentioned so far, this is the best tinder of all. You should always keep some in your survival kit. Seal the cloth, say bits ripped from an old shirt, in a tin can and keep it in the heart of the fire. The charred cloth which results is then ready to burst into flame at the touch of a spark.

ENERGY

Sugar is a source of instant energy which helps to produce body heat during an emergency camp. Oxo or bouillon cubes provide a hot, tasty drink that tastes like soup and warms the insides. It also helps to warm the inner body. And salt helps reduce tiredness, dehydration, and muscle cramps.

Pack half a dozen sugar cubes.

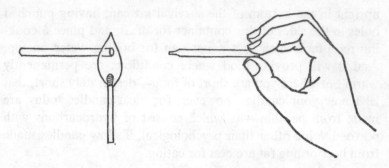

Salt in drinking straw

Cut an inch and a half from a drinking straw (the kind you drink Coke with). Touch one end quickly to a match flame. Nip the end together quickly with your fingers. It will remain sealed. Now tip a little heap of salt onto a sheet of paper. Fold the paper in half and pour the salt down the crease so it spills into the open end of the straw. When almost full, bring a match flame near this end of the straw and pinch smartly together between thumb and forefinger. Your salt will be safe.

Pack two or three *tea bags* inside the survival kit.

TOOLS

The thinnest variety of strong "hairy" string is best—especially for tying plastic to stones when making a shelter. It has many other uses, like snares and deadfalls, fishing lines and lashings for loads to be carried.

Thick fuse wire, or any thin strong wire, can bind a small penknife to a stick to make a spear. It will make snares when you *have* to live off the land and catch small animals for food. It is also useful as a handle for supporting your small tin can cooking pot—the survival kit container—over a hot fire.

Safety pins have hundreds of uses—from a makeshift fishing hook to the fastening for a piece of clothing which has ripped and which is letting in a deadly chill.

The lid of your tin can survival kit is easily made into a

flasher. A hole punched through the middle is the only requirement—although it should be of fairly bright metal too.

Choose a small penknife made from stainless steel. It should be kept sharp; keep it well oiled too. Large finger and thumb holes will help you to open it all the more easily when your fingers are wet and muddy. (Fingernails become softened in wet, cold conditions and may be unable to open up a stiff blade.) If there is no room in the tin, pack a sharp modeler's blade bought from a hobby shop.

Magnetize a large needle so it will always swing to the north when floated on a pool, or hung from a thread. (Never grip thread too tightly or its twist can distort where the needle eventually comes to rest—the pool method is best.) Paint the north-pointing end bright red so you don't forget. But how do you make the needle into a magnet? Easy—simply stroke the needle in one direction only with a pocket magnet. *Now check at home with a proper compass in the room. Whichever end of the needle keeps turning to north and resting in that position, that's the red end.* North. Pack a toy compass too as a double-check.

Tape, used to seal the tin can, can be used as emergency bandages, patches, etc. Buy the kind that can be used more than once. It's great for compressing plastic sheet into a tight bundle.

Toy balloon is great for carrying water in desert situations: you can blow the water into it by taking mouthfuls and spurting them through the length of straw that was used to carry the salt. Needs practice, but it can be done. It can also be used for signaling. And even to amuse yourself—this is not as funny as it sounds: keeping your sense of humor is a vital aspect of survival.

Whistle? Yes, pack a small one if there is room. But you should always carry a whistle anyway, separately in a pocket for emergencies. And you can make good whistles from twigs. (See chapter 7 on signaling.)

Finally, before sealing the tin can survival kit, remember to fill any spare space left over with food which has a high-energy content—like nuts, raisins, or barley sugar broken small. Skip pieces of broken-up chocolate, though—it melts in warm weather and clogs everything up. You will not be able to carry much food this way, but every little bit helps until you have found some "natural" food.

FOUNTAIN PEN SURVIVAL KIT

A fountain pen is a convenient kind of container. It is a familiar and handy shape, and you can wear it clipped over the edge of a pocket or lying flat inside. Small as it seems, such a container can hold enough to help you in the search for SHELTER, WARMTH, FOOD, and SIGNALING materials. However, in this instance you will need to improvise more.

The previous survival experiments were very necessary for the tin can survival kit to work. They are vital if you want your fountain pen kit to help you—for you are working with the very minimum of materials.

Buy a large, cheap plastic fountain pen—the fatter the barrel, the better. Remove the nib and filler part, so that the complete pen when screwed up again makes one long hollow space. Seal the tiny breathing holes in the barrel and cap by melting the plastic in a candle flame. When you have packed everything into this narrow tube, seal where the cap and barrel join with bright glo-colored sticky tape.

SHELTER

Details of how to make shelters from the land itself are given in the next chapter. The fountain pen kit, however, helps you to succeed here by giving you warmth and energy while you work.

WARMTH

Make a bonfire as described above.

Matches

Push the match heads (there should be about ½ inch of matchstick left on each) down the center of a drinking straw—the same kind as you used to pack salt away in the tin can kit. Seal both ends with a match flame. But do place the match heads in the same order—always headfirst. This way there is no risk of two match heads accidentally rubbing together and setting you on fire. Make the pipeline rather shorter than length of pen. The straw itself can be set on fire if you are desperate for tinder. It burns fast.

Birthday Cake Candle

Such a candle will fit nicely into the fountain pen; it will prove invaluable as a firelighter, as long as you don't waste the little there is through lack of practice. "Magic" birthday candles bought from a novelty store are effective too; if the wind blows one out it will still relight itself. And go on doing so until it burns itself out.

ENERGY

Pack this by pouring sugar into the pen's barrel and cap just before screwing them up. Then when you use the survival kit you only need unscrew the cap and tip the sugar into the palm of your hand. The fact that there is really very little to eat is not as important as the good you feel it will do you when facing hardship.

Make a short version of the ballpoint container already described to hold salt.

TOOLS

Having slipped the pipeline of matches inside the pen barrel, also drop the following items inside:

* a small magnetized needle.
* two tiny safety pins (the smallest are gold-colored).
* a small best-quality modeling-knife blade—the bent kind will stay sharper and stands less chance of snapping when you need it. If you cannot find one small enough, a pencil-sharpener blade will suffice. The two small safety pins can be clipped crosswise to each other through the hold in the blade to make good grippable "handlebars." Just a little experimenting will give you the right idea.

(Now drop the mini-tube of salt inside, and tuck the birthday candle into the top of the barrel.) Squeeze coils of thin tube wire next to the candle and matches pipeline in the mouth of the barrel. And fold a piece of foil about ¾″ square around the matches, candles, and wire—your sun flasher for SOS.

WHEN THE SURVIVAL KIT
IS INADEQUATE

What happens when your survival kits just aren't enough to cope? You have run out of matches, the candle has long been finished, the fuse wire lost, the last-ditch emergency rations eaten, and the knife blade is now blunt beyond belief . . . or perhaps your survival kits are brand-new yet they still seem hopelessly puny to deal with the crisis. For example, the young survivor struggling against all odds to erect a makeshift shelter for the night is going to despair if he is depending on his small penknife to hack down thick enough branches. It

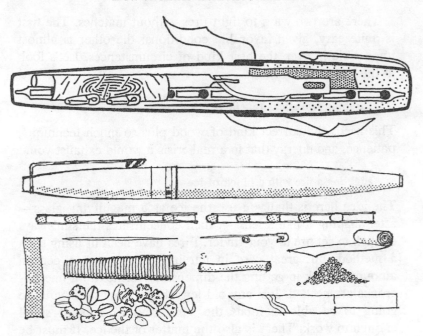

Fountain pen survival kit

will be far too small. There is only one answer. You must improvise with whatever materials are at hand.

Let me give you some examples. Suppose you have lost your compass—then use your wrist watch to tell the approximate direction (and even then a wrist watch is not a vital piece of equipment.) (See chapter 8.) Similarly suppose that you have eaten your last remnants of food from the survival kits. What now? The answer is that by now you should have discovered plants, meat, and fish to be going on with. And in any case, people can survive whole weeks without food, painful though indeed it is. Now all these makeshift improvisation tactics will be demonstrated in the following pages in different survival experiments. First, though, let's look at one very important aspect of improvisation—what to do when your matches run out.

There are two ways to light fires without matches. The first is quite easy, given favorable conditions; the other is almost impossible in even the best kind of circumstances. Let's look at the last category first.

Rubbing two sticks together

This needs the correct kind of wood plus so much technique, patience, and energy that in a real crisis it would exhaust you.

Lighting a fire with a block of ice

The idea here is that you use the ice as a magnifying glass— after shaping it like a lens—which concentrates the sun's rays enough to set fire to your tinder. Fires have been lit using such a method, but great care in carving the ice and a certain amount of luck in getting the dimensions formed to a fine tolerance are needed. Just any old lens shape won't do if you are going to be able to focus the sun's rays to a point small enough to work. There is also the matter of the ice. It must be as clear as glass. Ice from the freezer is no use, therefore, because it is too cloudy and full of internal striations. And it is rare that you will find any other ice so clear and yet of the right thickness—about an inch—capable of producing a flame. However, as we shall see in a moment, there are other ways of using the sun's power to ignite your tinder. But first there is one more method of lighting a fire which—while being quite possible—is nevertheless still difficult.

Making sparks

If you are playing darts and a dart bounces from the dartboard and hits a stone floor, you frequently see sparks; the same thing happens when someone wearing nailed boots or shoes is walking along a rocky track or hard road surface. (You see this best at night.) Any sharp object, such as a knife blade, for example, can be scraped on hard stone with the same result . . . sparks. Flint, obsidian, granite, and quartzite are typical examples of the kind of stone you need. As for the tinder, your piece of charred cloth mentioned earlier in this chapter is by far the best material to be ignited by the spark. Of course, it won't just burst into flames. You will see a glow as the spark catches, and then you must blow gently to fan it into flame.

And now for the fire lighting methods which don't need matches, and which are easier. Try all of these too as methods in actually lighting bonfires from glowing tinder.

Using a camera lens

A camera lens is the *best* lens for fire-starting, since it normally has a wider effective aperture than lenses used in other optical instruments. Simply open the iris diaphragm to the widest aperture, remove the back of the camera, and let the sun shine through the rear of the camera so the rays emerge from the front of the lens.

Using a spectacle lens

The single lens of a farsighted person can be used as a magnifying glass for the sun's rays. Experiment to find the best position as you hold it above the paper.

Flames from water

Buy two cheap identical watch crystals at a jeweler's Wait for strong sunshine. Pour a drop of water into one of the watch crystals, use the other as a lid (the crystals are now back to back), and smear a little chewing gum around the edges to make them stick. You now have a burning glass on the lines of that suggested by Jules Verne in *Dropped from the Clouds*. (His two watch crystals were sealed with clay.) Direct this makeshift lens so that the sun's rays converge through it in a sharp point on the tinder. Keep trying new positions with the

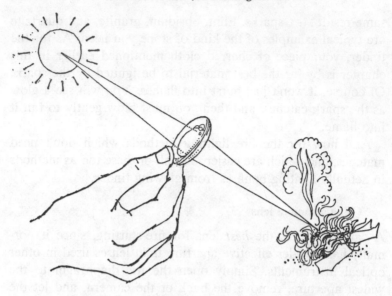

Fire from two watch crystals and water drop

lens until the tinder starts to smoke, then glow. Blow gently to produce a flame. Incidentally, one watch crystal on its own is not enough since it is then not a true lens, but a convex-concave lens which is useless.

Use a mirror as a burner

Any *concave* mirror like the inside of a car's headlights or a shaving mirror will concentrate the sun's rays into a burning spot of light that will ignite paper. It is important to focus these rays at a point about halfway between the center of curvature and the center of the mirror. The larger the size of mirror, the more powerful your fire-starter.

FINAL REMINDER

This book does NOT depend on survival kits to get you out of trouble. Rather, survival kits are very useful if you happen to

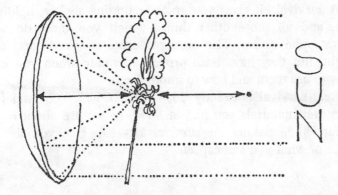

Fire from a concave car-headlight reflector or shaving mirror

have them with you in a crisis, but they are not indispensable. You should, for instance, always have them with you when experimenting in the tests given in this, and future, chapters, but were you to be caught out without a survival kit in a later and real life catastrophe, your training would stand you in good stead even though at first glance it seems you have absolutely nothing to help you.

And do remember: using SMALL survival kits involves a discipline where you must—but simply must—try out contents a number of times first to get the hang of operating everything. SMALL is really beautiful in this case for this very reason: it makes you intimately acquainted with survival kit contents. The person who carries a larger survival kit, full of impressive items like flashlight and SOS flares, tends to rely on the contents rather than on prior research, experiment, or practice using them, or in really trying to understand the principles behind them. It's so easy not to bother with the think-small, disciplined survival method which does give you that vital experience because it calls for a certain amount of effort from you. Consequently it gives you a head start when the chips are really down and it seems you have virtually nothing to aid you. But you do—you have self-knowledge based on past experiences.

A survival kit gives you grace in finding shelter, lighting a fire, and all those other things which you must do when catastrophe strikes. The extra resources it affords may seem slight, but they have been proved adequate when you know how to use them and how to improvise.

Real survival is exactly this—*IMPROVISING*. And from whatever materials you find at hand, as we are about to see. Meanwhile, making the survival kits can give you the first taste of what you can expect.

4

KEEPING WARM
IN A CATASTROPHE

Intense cold can kill before, it seems, you have been given even half a chance in survival crises outdoors. Ask any survivor who has experienced cold so bitter it curls up the body with its intensity; cold so knife-edged it glues your skin to any bare metal you touch (and though you snatch your body away, the skin remains stuck to the steel, wire, or whatever); cold so excruciating it makes the feeling in your fingers vanish and you have to wind your wrist watch with your teeth . . . and you will know only half the rigors of Arctic-type hardship. For a beginning, though, you could not do better than borrow from your local library Apsley Cherry-Garrard's *The Worst Journey In the World* and a short story by Jack London called "To Build a Fire." You will then have an inkling of the worst to expect.

Now, the cold you are going to have to contend with in bad situations is unlikely to be so severe, although it will certainly feel so at the time. Cold does not have to be that far below freezing point to be able to kill, especially when you compound its potential, terrible effects with overconfidence, casualness, and incompetence. Cold may be only the chill of evening drawing in, but if the weather is worsening, if a companion is injured, if you are lost in the wilderness, if you have mislaid important equipment, if you have somersaulted down the snow funnel of a mountainside, or if you are trapped up a tree by a vicious animal, it might still be a summer's day but the evening's cold you are about to face could kill you. So much depends on where you are and who you are.

First, however, you need to know how to live through the immediate crisis long enough to remain alive for when help finally does arrive. You have to keep warm right now in order to be able to signal help at the first opportunity. Succumb to the cold in the slightest way, and you are finished—or as good as.

You will need to work fast; blizzard, thunderstorm, gales, and penetrating cold will quickly bring you to the point of exhaustion. But any deterioration in weather, no matter how slight, brings a similar risk and an exhausted person will quickly become an exposure victim in bad weather.

The two priorities in fighting off the cold are SHELTER and WARMTH. However, before dealing with these, there are also two stages of simple experiments which should convince you of the full effects of cold in the Great Outdoors and how to fight it best by actually knowing your enemy.

STAGE ONE

Whenever you are out in the open, there is always a risk that body heat will be stolen. If it is cold *and* wet *and* windy, then beware! People not wearing proper clothing and who are unaware of the killer potential of such conditions could suffer from hypothermia[1] or exposure. This means that vital body heat leaks away, and you are literally chilled to the core—the *body's* core. Your brain knows this and does all it can to preserve a central core of warmth deep inside you. Try this experiment.

Touch a block of ice and watch your nerves turn off the

[1] See special note on pages 172–73

flow of warm blood to the chilled hand. This is to stop too much cold blood returning in a rush to the heart.

Shivering is good for you. The muscle spasms which shake you in shivering are really a highly sophisticated method of internal central heating. It is the body's way of keeping you warm. Not only are your muscles richly fed with warm blood, their movement actually generates heat. Doctors know that under average conditions, muscles make enough heat to boil a quart of iced water every hour. And when you stamp your boots or flap your arms you are stoking up the furnace of your muscles. Stand around in the frost, however—especially if you are inadequately protected and exhausted—and your muscles will take over and warm themselves by shivering. As for goose pimples—they are caused by the hair-erecting muscles in the skin contracting with the cold. So how well you survive cold temperature boils down to how well you make use of the body's canny way of fighting the cold.

The body can only control our bodily temperature so far, however. If you are too casual, then you will aid elements which attack your system.

A good example of this is in wearing the wrong kind of clothing while doing these wintry experiments. Experienced outdoorsmen always advise beginners to wear *loose-fitting wool clothing*. If you doubt this hint, try these experiments and see for yourself.

Immerse the sleeve end of a cotton shirt, and another of a woolen sweater, into a frying pan containing an inch of water. Watch how the cotton picks up the water very quickly, and how the cloth remains wet. The wool gets wet only where it is in the water. Moreover, wool has the unique property of retaining body warmth *even* when wet. It dries fast, sheds water, and traps a layer of warm air around your body.

Pull a wool sock over one hand and a cotton one over the other. Dip both hands in cold water, and dry them by swinging both fists through the air. The wool sock dries far quicker than the cotton sock, and never feels really cold. The cotton sock, however, stays damp and clammy.

Wet clothing is especially dangerous in winter because it allows vital body warmth to escape more than two hundred times faster than dry clothing.

Hold your head out through the open window of a moving car. It quickly feels numb, caused by the fast-moving air which slashes across it. Now, lick a hand and rub it across both eyes. The speeding air at once stings and smarts that part of the face in just the same way that wind blowing across snow bites into bodies that are not properly clothed, *and which are also wet.* And you do get wet in snow—from condensing perspiration; from falling into snowdrifts and quite possibly slipping into freezing water, too; from the sudden icy rain which lashes across the snow slope; and from steady snow falling through the late afternoon.

STAGE TWO

The answer—and this includes questions you may pose while making any one of the snow shelters described below—is that you should dress in *layers* of clothing which trap layers of dead air in between each garment, and so insulate you from the cold most effectively because heat travels very slowly through still air. You can then peel them off or put extra ones on, depending on the weather conditions at the time. Several thin woolen sweaters (always better than a couple of thick, chunky ones) are the ideal—protected by a windproof and waterproof parka, jacket, or cagoule of plastic or rubberized nylon. Always carry windproofs with you. These items are lightweight and inexpensive. Do not consider just the top garments either—windproof trousers are also necessary.

Assuming you are now safely clad, there is still one area of the body which is vulnerable—the head. The mountaineer's saying, "When your feet are cold, wear a hat," is all too true.

It should be a balaclava, preferably. And your parka, jacket, or cagoule should have a hood which can be pulled over the woolen hat.

The back of the head and nape of the neck are the most vulnerable parts of the upper half of the body, where heat can trickle away. So wear a scarf.

Then there are the wrists, hands, and kneecaps. You must protect them from the cold: the hands and wrists with warm mittens (keep in mind the saying of Polar explorers who claim that if you lose your gloves, you also lose your life in extreme cold); the kneecaps with warm wool trousers (and possibly long johns underpants and waterproof leggings as well).

Experiment with these different pieces of clothing on the different parts of your body in varying temperatures as you travel through wild country. There is nothing like the personal experience of having felt the chill that occurs through wearing only two thick sweaters on a cold day, when three or four thin wool sweaters would make you feel twice as comfortable. Of course, for safety reasons, you should have those lighter wool sweaters in your rucksack while actually trying out the inferior thick sweaters—then, if it really does get a lot colder, you are literally covered because you have the correct wear in reserve. Another miniature hell you can discover for yourself is to walk in jeans on a wet and windy day. You will soon see just how quickly the wind races through the damp material and steals your body heat. Again, have the correct back-up wear of woolen long johns, wool trousers, and rainproof over-trousers with you in a rucksack and keep to a low-level hike of roughly 1,000 feet. Then again, some other time walk for as long as you can on a cold day without eating anything. Make it a low-level hike for safety's sake and have the kind of quick-energy food already mentioned packed away at the bottom of your rucksack. When you are starting to feel really weary—eat. The difference in your morale and progress will be startling. Compare those hours when you went hungry with the next day's progress when you continually chew at nuts, raisins, and chocolate; your performance will be so much better in every respect.

Sustain the warmth deep inside you with food. Do this while making whatever snow shelter you happen to choose. Develop the habit, and nibble the food throughout any day spent in the outdoors. Chewing small amounts of food gives a valuable source of heat. Sweets are quickly converted into energy—nuts, cheese, chocolate, raisins, dates, and flapjacks will also help to keep you warm. There is no doubt that such food really does help to boost energy and stave away exhaustion, for lack of zest and fatigue are usually the first signs that a person is suffering from mild hypothermia which can rapidly grow worse . . . of which more later.

Now is the time to go into the two priorities which are necessary if you do meet with catastrophe. Making shelters is the first, and it has a direct bearing on those experiments which we have just considered.

SHELTER

It is of vital importance to stay warm when lost or stranded. Therefore, making some sort of shelter is the first priority for anyone in trouble deep in wild country.

No one who has built several shelters from snow need ever come to serious harm in a blizzard. Snow is a great insulating material that keeps you warm and safe. Once again, here is another example of still air proving an ideal insulator from the freezing cold. The pocket of dead air within your snow shelter is thus easily warmed with your body heat.

Although many people associate snow with winter tragedies, it is a real safeguard in times of emergency. A lighted candle, for example, is all that is required to heat and light a small snow shelter. Regardless of how cold it is outside, the temperature inside a well-constructed snow cave will not fall much below −10° F. (−23° C.) even though it could well be −50° F. (−45° C.) outside. Your body heat alone can raise the temperature of a snow shelter by as much as 45° F. (7° C.).

Try the following experiments in hacking out different kinds of refuge from blizzard or bitter cold the next time you have a good fall of snow.

Survival snow cave

Tunnel upward into a deep snowdrift at right angles to the wind. Just burrow a hole big enough to get into. A small snow hole will be warmer than a large one. It will take about four hours for two people equipped with improvised digging implements to hack out a small snow cave which is cozy and warm. Such make-do shovels can be made from ice axes, large chunks of tree bark, branches, rocks, skis, climbers' crash helmets, and so on.

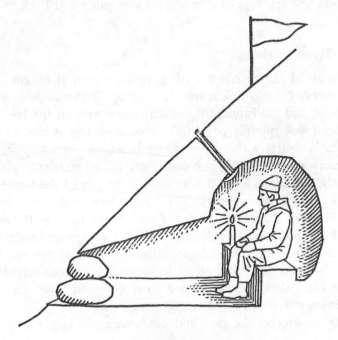

Snow cave

Scrape the snow from the hole first. Then, lift the snow away in blocks. If the snow is so soft that the blocks crumble, the temperature is too warm to cement such a snow cave solid. Make the cave bigger from the inside. Shape the roof and walls with a piece of branch or rock so that moisture does not drip and chop a roomy bench just beneath the ceiling where the air is warmest.

Punch a ventilation hole in the roof. Keep it open by ramming a stick through it occasionally—and leave the stick in place so that a draft blows down it. The doorway should never be blocked completely. Leave a small opening so that fresh air keeps circulating. This is VERY important.

If you have to go outside in the blizzard—were this a real emergency—knot a piece of brightly colored clothing to the end of the stick and push it through the ventilation hole before you leave. The flag will help to guide you back to the cave.

Tree pit shelter

This could not be simpler—it is just the natural hollow in a snowdrift from which a tree is growing. If the snow is deep enough and the funnel-shaped depression around the trunk is defined well enough, you will be able to enlarge it into a comfortable shelter with only a moderate amount of scooping out of snow needed. Just climb down into it, and start enlarging it on the lee side. Throw the snow onto the rim of the funnel to make a higher windbreak. The roof is best made from limbs and boughs. Any large pieces of bark found lying in the snow will also provide valuable insulation. An evergreen-bough bed shields you from the cold ground and general dampness. It is worth taking time and effort to make this as comfortable as possible. Select boughs from a tree at ground level, possibly the very tree which is the center of your pit.

Work around the tree and cut boughs no larger than the

ubiquitous ball point. Gather enough to make a bed at least 10 in. (25 cm.) thick and surround the base of the trunk with small logs or rocks. The fir boughs are arranged against these, radiating around in rows with the cut-off ends to the ground and the tip ends toward the tree. Coniferous boughs have springy curves. The convex side of this bend should face upward to give the bed its bounciness. Continue the rows laid overlapping each other to make a mattress from wall to wall. Add extra boughs where needed after giving the bed a "comfort test" by sitting and lying on it. Incidentally, holly also makes a springy extra for any snow cave bed.

It is amazing how warm and cozy—even without any form of heating—such a tree pit shelter can be when floored and roofed with evergreen branches.

Snow basement

You can dig a snow hole like a trench in fairly level snow, then cover it with large snowballs. This type of shelter is a lot quicker and easier to make than an igloo. It will not look so good, but it will keep you warm.

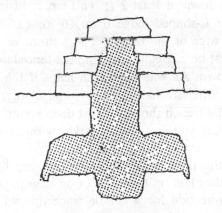

Snow basement

Having reached the bottom of the trench at a depth of 5 ft. or 6 ft. (2 m.), cut into one or both of the long sides to make chambers. You will be able to sit in these recesses, after first carving out a platform with a gutter around the edges to drain away condensation.

The top of the trench can be sealed with large snowballs rolled from the snow you lifted out of the channel. Press the snowballs tightly together. Cement the chinks with small snowballs. Leave one big ball of snow free to move as the "trap door"—to be rolled aside when you drop in and climb out.

Snow tent

Scuff out a trench in the snow about 3 ft. (90 cm.) across, and a little longer than the length of your body, with the heel of a boot. If you found it difficult to scratch an impression on the surface of the snow, you can continue—the snow is hard enough.

Cut the slabs for the sides of the tent about 6 in. (15 cm.) thick. Lay them aside as you move them carefully from the trench. Dig down at least 2 ft. (60 cm.), lifting more slabs. Next cut an L-shaped ledge 6 in.×6 in. (15 cm.×15 cm.) along each edge of the trench. The bottom of the tent's side slabs will rest here. Begin propping the tent slabs against each other as shown. As you can see, it helps if the placing of the slabs is off-center so that you need handle only one snow slab at a time. The trench should be just deep enough and the slabs so angled that you can sit up inside without bumping your head.

Insulate the floor with evergreen boughs, holly branches, and old clothes laid on the snow or on newspapers. Scoop out a shelf on one side for a candle since this will give enough heat for comfort when both ends are *partially* blocked with snow—"partially," so there is straight-through ventilation.

The best entrance and exit is to use an end slab as a door. This is pulled into place from the inside—and pushed aside too.

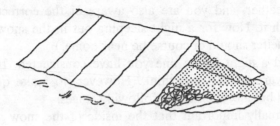

Snow tent

WARNING: While a blanket of snow is exactly that—a blanket which will protect you —it must be freezing for an ALL-SNOW shelter to be successful. Roofs and walls of snow caves need to be at least 2 ft. (60 cm.) thick in order to give you enough insulation and so they won't collapse. Wet snow IS unsuitable. Unless the temperature is below freezing a snow roof will fall down.

Hints on digging and using snow shelter

It is worth knowing how to dig—and not only in a proper emergency. It will make your snow shelter experiments much easier, and limit the risk of your pulling a muscle. Work slowly and not energetically. Aim to preserve strength. Take a break every few minutes and stop altogether if you feel tired. It is best to dig before eating or not less than two hours after a large meal. Use the whole body, too, as you work. Begin from the legs, and use the back muscles—getting all your weight behind your digging implement. Never maneuver it with arm power alone. And, although you will have stripped off your outer clothing, don't go to extremes and wear too few clothes: this can lead to chills. Avoid lifting too much snow at once— wet snow is heavier than the powdery kind, especially if you are using a heavy object to dig with. So you know the risks of cold weather, and you are also aware of the correct way to live with it. Now for a night sleeping out in the snow. (Your snow shelter should of course be near home.)

Spend a night in the one you have constructed. It will be much warmer than you think. However, to make quite sure you will be safe, stick to the following stages.

It is really important that the inside of the snow shelter is kept as dry as possible. Shake out any clothing that has snow sticking to it before entering—the snow melts and forms puddles. Stamp the floor flat. Blot up any water dripping from the roof or down the sides of the shelter with bits of snow.

Although you will need to build up snow in the entrance once you are inside—roll big snowballs there, for example— remember to leave a hole so there is a draft of fresh air.

Never sit down directly onto snow; cover the bench you cut with evergreen boughs, old newspapers, or a piece of spare clothing; you don't need to wear ALL your clothes inside the snow refuge.

Avoid using a stove that will make the temperature rise and which will make the roof drip. Limit cooking to warming up food and water over a candle—this way you cut down on steam. Cooking over a candle? Yes. If you have more than one tin can, stick a candle in the snow. Place one tin can with bottom and top removed over it. (The tin can should also have a number of holes punched in the sides with a nail.) Using another slightly larger tin you can heat enough water to make soup, as well as other dehydrated packet foods—ideal for your experimental night out in a snowdrift.

Protect your sleeping bag from the snow floor with evergreen boughs, etc. (just as you padded the bench where you have been sitting).

Keep an ice ax, thick branch, or whatever you dug your

snow shelter with inside in case the roof falls in and you have
to dig your way out.

OTHER SURVIVAL SHELTERS

There are many different kinds of shelters possible when, at
first glance, it seems there is nothing. Remember, you can
always gain protection from wind, cold, rain, or tremendously
hot sun beneath any ready-made natural shelter. Below trees,
logs, rocks, cliffs—any place with a lee side to protect the
body from the elements. If you are among trees, for instance,
the quickest, easiest, and least energy-burning form of shelter
is the downed tree with space between the trunk and the
ground. Lean branches and logs on both sides of the trunk to
form a crude type of roof and wriggle beneath. For the
moment you are safe.

Downed tree shelter

A universal refuge in wild country is the barn. Today, however, the hay which can make all the difference between life
and death to a freezing person is usually no longer loose.

It is mostly stacked in hard-packed bales and you cannot wrap up in these, so you have to undo two or three of these bales first and shake the hay free. Cut the string which ties the bales on any sharp edge you can find—a rusty nail, sickle, or whatever—and peel apart the compressed wads of hay until you can shred it into small pieces with your fingers. Then, burrow beneath it where the warmth lies. Only do this, however, when you really are in trouble—not now as a survival experiment.

Instead, try this one. It can house you in a crisis or, perhaps, protect someone who is injured and waiting for a rescue team to come. And the principle behind its construction can be applied to other shelters using different materials—there is no end to the designs of domes you can dream up.

Survival dome

First, scavenge for really long willow wands. Then, scratch out a rough outline of the foundation of the dome; it can be oval, round, or even square. Its width, however, should not measure much more than the average length of your willows.

Push the thick end of a wand into the ground at a point somewhere on your scratched-out outline. Stick in another wand at a point opposite on the outline—again, the thick end being buried in the ground. Draw the two tops together over the center of the site you selected, and tie them with roots, shoelaces, or anything else handy.

Now fix, bend, and tie another pair of wands so that they cross the center of the dome's site and also cross the first arch at right angles. Lash all four wands together at this point. The curve of the dome's ceiling is now seen, and future arches to be made will be smaller. A short distance away from the first arch, for example, build a slightly lower arch that is parallel to the first. Cross this at right angles with a similar arch. Continue this latticework—ensuring good lashings—until the frame resembles a large sturdy wickerwork basket turned upside down. All the joints that cross are tied securely. The only break is the space left for a door.

Moss, grass, bracken, leaves, nettles (grip by pressing hard on the stem and leaves between finger and thumb so they do not sting you), heather, and straw can all be woven through the finished basketlike shape. You can also plaster thick mud and snow over the framework.

The most universal kind of shelter is a roof which leans up against some solid support. It could be branches slanted up against a wall or boulder, or small logs and pieces of bark which are tilted against a fallen tree trunk (and you lie or sit in the space beneath the trunk and the propped-up lean-to sides). There is plenty of scope for invention here. As long as the doorway of your lean-to shed faces away from the wind and as long as you make a well-woven rainproof roof, you will be quite safe beneath its shelter.

Such a shelter need not be elaborate. Keep it simple, especially for the first night were you really caught out in a survival situation. A very simple shed will still shield you from wind and rain. However, if you have to stay, make it more draftproof, and build a fire near the opening so that the heat is bounced back toward the shelter with a reflector.

WARNING: Be careful in woodland when experimenting with shelter construction. Landowners will take exception to your stripping trees bare. Use dead and fallen branches and natural covering lying on the ground.

Your shed bed can be made on the same principles as described in the Tree Pit Shelter. Lay out pine needles, evergreen boughs, grass, heather, dry moss, and bracken for as thick and springy a mattress as possible. Aim to make it at least a foot thick—and don't forget that holly is excellent as a base for your outdoor bed. Do not just make the shelter during the day. Sleep in it at night—during the summer—without a sleeping bag or blankets. But more of this later.

Now try a test at home in your garage, and experience how you can become warm in conditions that you would normally consider far too chilly.

It need not be midwinter; you can do experiments at any time of year. It does, however, underline a very important principle of winter survival—namely:

NEVER leave a snowbound car stuck in isolation among snowdrifts in a blizzard—unless you know exactly where you are going. If you do abandon the car, and then get lost, you will probably never find the car again. Now without any form of shelter, you will stand every chance of succumbing to the cold and snowfall, exhausted. Always stay with a snowbound car.

Carry out the drill now. Sleep on the back seat after winding down the window an inch (you would do this in a snow survival scene too) for ventilation. Light a candle and place it on the sill beneath the rear window. This is all the heat you require. In a real-life outdoor situation the driver of the car would be able to run the motor in bursts through the night providing he had enough gasoline and could keep the exhaust free and so keep the heater pumping out hot air. Of course you must never run the motor in a garage; if you fall asleep in the car, then there is more than a risk of carbon monoxide poisoning from the exhaust fumes. However, you can store heat your own way now—and grow warmer too.

WARMTH

We have shelter now. There is still no guarantee, however, that in a real emergency we shall also have a sleeping bag, extra clothing or even—as we hope—a fire. It is always a tragedy when potential survivors have successfully built a shelter . . . only for them to be still beaten by the cold as the night air freezes and the ground crackles with frost.

The following heat-giving experiments will help you to experience a glow throughout your body. And with any luck you will have a fire too. (See chapter 3.)

Practice body-heating where you are. You may be waiting for a train and your teeth are chattering, or perhaps you are watching a football game and can no longer feel your toes. Imagine you are sitting on a mountain ledge during an all-night bivouac and just waiting for the dawn so that you can begin climbing again at the point where oncoming night had stopped you. Try whichever of the following experiments are suitable at any time.

It is worth noting that in all these experiments, however, you must *think* too. Your physical movements in keeping warm must be properly mentally controlled. Why? Because the *correct* conservation of body energy and body heat is essential. In cold areas—just one example—it pays not to sweat, because wet inner clothes can freeze. Moisture is *the* biggest problem in keeping warm in cold weather. Slow down body movements therefore. And think: "Brute strength is a disadvantage in a blizzard."

Here are other key facts too—if you are outdoors and the temperature is less then 98° F. (37° C.) (body temperature), do NOT waste muscular energy, touch anything colder than 98° F. (37° C.) if you can help it, or stand still and let the wind whisk your body heat away. Or you really will leak energy and become colder deep inside you—where it matters most.

Keep shoes together and hop up and down without stopping. You will begin to feel warm. If this were a real emergency, remember one thing—that you can jump too vigorously. Energetic movements burn up energy inside you which is needed for maintaining that inner core of body warmth.

Curl and uncurl fingers and toes—even when you cannot feel them. Do not stop when the warmth begins to return, even though it is painful.

Let your body shake in spasms—it is part of Nature's way of warming the body. Do not try to stop it.

Breathe warm air onto your fingers until they begin to thaw —and it hurts. By blowing into a cupped hand held in front of the mouth you can also warm your face.

Pummel and slap your body, crossing your arms over. Pummel and slap friends too!

Make as many different faces as you can before your face feels numb . . . and especially when it does. It is easy to be frostbitten on this exposed area of skin. So keep it mobile.

Push your hands below your armpits when very cold— beneath your clothing. Or force them down inside the front of your underpants between your legs. These are the two warmest parts of the body for hand-warming. Your mouth is good too for fingertips.

Nick a tiny hole near the cuff of each sleeve of whatever garment has the longest sleeves. (It may be a sweater, say, worn under a windbreaker, or it may be the windbreaker.) The holes should be on the inside of the sleeves so that you can stick your thumbs through them. This holds down the sleeves over your hands when you have no gloves.

Wear Wellington boots?—then pack hay around the insides around your legs. You will immediately feel warm. Pine boughs can have the same effect.

Snowflakes stick to clothing and make it wet. Brush away any particles of snow or ice before they melt when entering a snow shelter. And do not sit down on, or lean directly against, snow.

Take off your top garments—jacket AND raincoat, for example—and wrap them around your shoulders without pushing your arms down the sleeves. Then button up the front. This will hold a layer of warm air around you—fed by your body heat.

Wrap newspaper around your body, packing the layers in between whatever clothes you have on. Push newspaper down the waistband of your trousers, up your trouser cuffs, and inside your sleeves—as well as around your torso.

Do not have anything too tight—shoelaces? waistband of trousers? collar? Check and undo to assist your circulation.

Paper bags stuffed with hay, straw, grass, ferns, or whatever help as makeshift gloves.

Turn sweaters around so the front of your neck is protected by the back of a V-necked sweater. Meanwhile your coat or jacket shields the V section now at the back.

Push shirt and sweaters down inside your underpants, then fasten up your trousers again. But do not pull the belt too tight on these extra thicknesses of material.

These experiments will help keep and restore the body's warmth without actually increasing it a great deal—though it feels like it as the ends of your fingers begin to tingle.

Here is an experiment for the hardy who have a shallow

pond or stream near home. There is no need for the less tough to try it, however. Just know what to do. The experiment will make your whole body glow like toweling yourself briskly after a cold shower. Wear *woolen* clothing—trousers, shirt, and one or two sweaters—and jump into the water, letting your whole body get a soaking. Jump out quickly and throw yourself onto the snow by the side of the water. Still with your clothing on, roll over several times until you begin to feel warm. It is not only your exertions which are heating you, though. The snow helps to absorb the moisture in your clothing and dries you out too. If you leap up and down now and then—thumping off lumps of damp snow sticking to you—and then selecting a fresh patch of snow in which to roll, you will become even warmer. This is the practice of aircraft pilots who crash-land in the Arctic, and who are unlucky enough to land in water. It works.

If you did not do this, and had slipped into the icy water during a cross-country trek in winter, you would risk falling prey to frostbite *and* hypothermia. This would be because of the combination of wet clothing plus a cold wind freezing you.

If you become frostbitten you will be able to treat yourself before it has gained a good hold. Otherwise it is a matter for a doctor. The early stages of frostbite are when the cold first *nips* you, and the signs are a loss of feeling in that part of the body as well as waxy-looking skin. If you look at the immediate case history of what you suspect is frostnip, you can also get a clue. Suppose your feet felt numb after walking through snow for several hours in tightly laced boots—then that is probably your answer: The boots were so tight they cut off the circulation, and the cold has started to attack. Or you might have been walking along a snow-covered track in light shoes. Well, that is reason enough to frostnip your toes severely. Then, again, your face could become frostnipped if it has been exposed to a freezing wind for a long time.

There is really no excuse for becoming a frostnip victim if you wear adequate clothing for the surroundings and time of year. And if you are on your guard from the beginning so that even if you do suffer from the opening stages of frostbite through no fault of your own, you can tackle them before they grow too serious and need medical attention fast.

What you must NOT do is: apply gasoline, alcohol, or kerosene to the suspected frostbite, rub snow on the affected part, chafe the deadened skin in any way, or try direct warmth from a bonfire, lighter, or candle flame. ALL are dangerous.

The remedy for frostbite is much more simple *as long as you catch it in the reasonably early stages.* Treat the affected limbs or body parts with human warmth. It can be your own warmth or that of another person. If your face is so numb that you cannot feel part of it, then cover that part with the warmth of a hand (making sure you cover the back of the hand with a piece of clothing so that it, in turn, does not become affected by the cold). Hold the warm palm against your face until you begin to feel the pain of warmth returning to the frost-pinched piece of skin. It will be painful; don't be surprised. If, instead, your toes are numb and the skin looks waxy—place them in someone else's clothing so that they rest against their stomach or under one of their armpits. Both of these places give a human warmth which can save your toes. As for frozen fingers, either push them down the front of your trousers into the warmth between your legs, or press them beneath your own armpits. Hold them there until you gain feeling in them once more. For hypothermia, see special note on pages 172–73. It can affect you at any time of the year.

5

SURVIVAL JOURNEY ON LAND

So far we have dealt with the immediate action to take in the most common kinds of outdoor emergency, where shelter and warmth are vital. Statistics do, in fact, show that more accidents happen through a combination of bad weather and getting lost than any other way. There are, however, many exigencies in outdoor-survival situations where the first imperative is SPEED. You must know what to do, and speed is of the essence—just as a racing driver learns to steer instinctively away from a potential crash only a split second away. You may not be a Grand Prix driver, but you could be faced one day with an inrushing tide which is pinning you against sea cliffs on a remote coast, and you need to get higher as fast as you can.

Whatever your kind of shelter, you will need SPEED—in a tent or in an emergency snow bivouac which has already saved you from a bad situation—when your ventilation fails. Never sit back in any form of living quarters out-of-doors without checking this—know the danger.

The danger is quite simple, but by the same token it is all the more deadly for it. All it needs is for your stove to burn steadily away in a closed tent, and there is a build-up of carbon monoxide—a killer gas—which induces drowsiness and a desire to sleep. Many young campers have died because they did not check to see if their tents had *two* vents by which fresh air could circulate while they cooked after a hard day's walking, climbing, canoeing. The worse the weather too, the more likely the tent is to be zipped up tight, increasing the need for adequate ventilation.

Besides feeling drowsy there is another sign which shows the presence of carbon monoxide. If your cooker is burning with a *yellow* flame, open the door as fast as you can. *Only the healthy blue flame is safe.* And do not regard this as being a warning for campers only. There is as much danger of a carbon monoxide build-up in any confined spaces—like snow holes, for instance. Wherever you are cooking, sleeping, and living in the outdoors, you must have through ventilation.

LIGHTNING

It is not necessary to throw away metal pieces of equipment like ice axes, karabiners, rucksacks, and crampons. They do not attract lightning any more than you do, and you could meet serious trouble by throwing away vital gear.

However, you should know the places to stay away from when lightning is about . . . and the spots to head for where safety is virtually assured.

Worst places	Best places
Beneath oak, poplar, or elm trees whose sap blows up if struck by a lightning flash.	In the midst of dense woods where all the trees are more or less the same height—you would have to be very unlucky for it to strike the tree under which you are immediately sheltering.
Anywhere where you are the tallest and most obvious silhouette against open country . . . and the lightning flash is only five seconds be-	

fore the crash of thunder (divide the number of seconds by five to find how many miles away the lightning is striking): in this case it is only one mile away, too near for comfort.

Beneath an isolated tree, no matter how tall. Or below any other high-standing targets which, by their lonesome height, attract lightning flashes. (The Empire State Building in New York City has been struck many times a year because it stands so much higher than the other tall buildings around it.)

Cave entrances: they pull lightning because of the ionization of the air at the cave mouth.

Mountain skylines—especially in overcast, rainy weather.

Steep hillsides, rock-face cracks, and rock overhangs . . . steer clear of these spots even though they would appear to give welcome shelter. For example,

Inside a car whose surface distributes the lightning through its metal and then guides it back to earth.

Inside any building which has a "low profile" because it is among other buildings in the immediate neighborhood. And is of much the same height.

Lying on your stomach in the middle of a field and thereby presenting a low profile. If you were standing up, you would then be in one of the worst places.

Sitting on an open scree slope well below mountain crests and well away from any rock faces—knees up and with your hands in your lap. Crouch, squatting on the balls of your feet, if you have rubber-soled boots.

if you crouch beneath a roof formed by a ledge of jutting granite, then you are in a very dangerous position. A flash of lightning could strike the projecting lip of the overhang and then, at once, begin arcing to the ground beneath. You, trapped in the middle, will be in the position of being electrocuted in a giant spark plug. Yet, it was that projection of the overhang which attracted the lightning in the first place.

Anywhere flat where you can lie, crouch, or sit. Do not worry if your ice ax is making a buzzing sound, your hair is standing on end, your eyebrows are tingling, and there are blue flashes all over the ground in front of your eyes. So long as you keep low and on the level, the big forks of lightning will most likely miss you, even though the immediate atmosphere is highly charged with electricity.

CLIMBING IN EMERGENCIES

Climbing higher to a ledge above the tide now racing up the beach; clawing a way across a wet and greasy rock slab that runs across a mountain track (with the penalty for a slip being an icy plunge down over sharp rocks); scrambling back up an icy hillside slope down which you have already fallen and landed unhurt—*and* night is drawing in fast. In all these instances speed is vital.

Do the climbing experiments listed below. They will give you a better insight into climbing, boost your confidence, and are fun to do.

Look for a low wall made out of stone or bricks—like the walls of your garden, perhaps, or a wall in the park, or in the grounds of a school. Wear rubber-soled shoes like training shoes or tennis shoes, and you are ready. No, the idea is not to

scale the wall from bottom to top—that would be too dangerous. Instead, climb two or three feet from the ground—certainly no more—and then climb sideways across the wall to
the left or to the right. The idea is to cross one side of a building, then without stepping down back onto the ground, traverse the next three sides as well until you have made a complete circuit and arrive back at the point from where you
began. Of course, you will face lots of minor tumbles when
your feet or fingers slip, but you are so near to the ground that
you can jump off without harm.

Remember; SPEED is the thing here. You are not practicing climbing for climbing's sake. You are testing yourself for
when you may have to scramble as high as you can as fast as
you can. Time your traversing circuits with a watch, and com-
pete against a friend. As long as you keep near the ground
there is no harm done. And this way, it does make you aware
of the different types of rock-face handholds and footholds
which are not obvious at first.

The edges of your shoes can be used on the smallest ledges
as long as you watch where you place your feet. The part that
climbers use most is the outer edge of the big toe. You must
learn to trust such seemingly nonexistent support and really
come to depend on your footwork. Keep the heels down; do
not put the weight of your body on your legs until you are
sure your shoes are placed just right and then—step up. Leg
muscles are more important than biceps in climbing. Your
hands and arms should be used only for balancing with as you
stand supported on your feet. If you search only for handholds—as you will quickly find—then the chances are you
will soon become spread-eagled, plastered against the wall of
the building and unable to go up or down—until you fall off.
Think of footholds instead.

However, you will also find different types of handholds—
varying from undercling holds, side holds, incut holds to pressure holds. The diagram will show exactly how you pull and
push on these aids . . . and these will be the type of holds you

Cat burglar's traverse

must use if ever you are in the predicament of having to climb up steep rock quickly.

Of course, the practice you gain here, should never be put into practice on real cliffs, unroped and just for kicks. Climbing an attractive sea cliff above a golden beach may seem irresistible when you are on vacation at the coast, but each year too many young people try the same thing, and either fall and injure themselves, or have to be rescued by the coast guards.

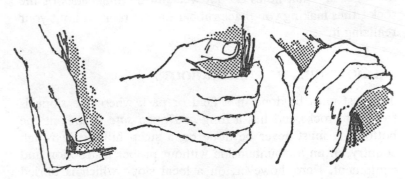

Climbing handholds

If you feel you really want to climb, then take a climbing course, join a mountain club, and learn to climb properly with a nylon rope and other correct accessories. The climbing practice suggested here is something you can do at home, and will give you basic experience in how to tackle an emergency—it does not give you a license to go rock climbing on your own for fun.

HOW TO STICK TO ROCKS BETTER

Wait for a rainy day, and try your climbing circuit around a building at low level, again with rubber-soled shoes. You will immediately find a big difference . . . your shoes skid and slip off the footholds. Well, this could happen in a real-life situation too. You may *have* to traverse greasy, oily, slippery, slimy, oozy rock on a mountain; the reason it is so treacherously lubricated is that when rock is mossy, rain will make it feel as if it has been squirted with an oilcan. The answer is to try your climbing circuit across the building's walls but in stockinged feet this time. It makes a tremendous difference and you have a much better grip even though it is uncomfortable. Then, try wearing your rubber-soled shoes with an old pair of socks pulled over them which is better still. There is just one danger: be sure—especially in a true-life situation of this kind—that holes do not wear in the undersides of the socks, thus making you place rubber on wet rock without your realizing it.

SKI DOWNHILL IN RUBBER BOOTS

This test must be done in a field or park where the slope is free from rocks and has a long and open *safe* runout at the bottom. It must never be done on a steep hillside in rough country, or on a mountainside without proper instruction and equipment. Here, however, on a local slope which is buried under hard-frozen snow, it will help to give you confidence on snow slopes. You never know when this experience will be useful. Many motorists have never been on a snow slope in their lives until the day their car plunges over the edge of a steep hill pass and rolls several hundred feet down the mountainside. In many cases the passengers in such vehicles survive the rolling-over-and-over of the car, but it is the climb back up the glittering icy snow slope which gets them.

The experiment is a sliding downhill one, but it teaches one important factor needed on steep-angled snow: *balance*. Trying to keep upright at first on a steep snow slope is like walking a high wire; your body tends to be all over the place, first one way, then the other. But a few slides downhill—or *glissades* as they are known to climbers—will make you more confident, and able to stand straight up on your feet in this unusual environment.

Any rubber-soled boots will do—even Wellington boots— as long as it is for practice on local and safe slopes. You need one more aid. Make an ice ax out of a tree branch. Look for a strong branch—thick and forked. The fork should jut back down like the spout of a soda siphon, and be only a few inches from the end of the otherwise smooth branch. Check that your branch is not dead, or it will snap.

Stand at the top of your slope. Place both boots together as if you are standing on skis. Press the soles against the snow, and push the toe of one boot just ahead of the other. If you now point the toes downward a little, and if the snow is hard enough, you will begin to slide.

And the correct position for your "ice ax?" Hold it across your body with the fork or "pick" (as it would represent on an actual ice ax) in one hand, but pointing downward. Your thumb should be hooked around the main length of the branch, just above the fork. The other hand should grasp the branch toward its other end, which is then trailed lightly in the snow. As you gather speed, make sure that your knees are flexed and that you keep your weight over the leading boot. You can now begin to turn in zigzags. Simply push the other boot forward instead and transfer your weight. By leaning out on the "ice ax" like a canoeist on his paddle, you are able to steer as you swap it from side to side, depending on which direction you wish to take.

To brake: dig in the end of the "ice ax." And your heels as well. If you fall, however, and the slope is so steep that you continue speeding downhill, you will be able to stop yourself in a flash by having already practiced the next experiment. It is a method which depends on your always carrying your ice ax with the "pick" part of it (see above) pointing down toward the ground.

If you ever find yourself on steep and hard-frozen snow slopes without an ice ax, you are in real trouble. An ice ax acts as a parachute if you fall. Anyone who does not have such an implement in his hands must find a makeshift one as quickly as possible. Although you could use the strong tree-branch ice ax used in the last experiment, you are unlikely to find a tree branch on mountains. In this case, you will have to use anything at all that is sharp pointed, and that can be held in the hands, so that if you slip you can drive it into the snow at once. It could be a chunk of rock, or even a bunch of keys gripped in your fingers so that the biggest key sticks out of your fist, but it must be something which you can jab into the snow and which could slow you down in your headlong flight.

There are right and wrong ways of sticking your ice ax into the snow, and the best way to find out is to make a fast glissade—once you have got the hang of the method—down a steep slope, and suddenly, deliberately, get out of control. Drop down onto the snow. It helps if you are wearing a nylon anorak or parka, because then the slippery garment will increase your speed down the safe slope, and that is what you want in order to make this test realistic . . . speed. Now, at first, it is unlikely that you can pull up from your downward rush before reaching the bottom of the slope, unless you brake the correct way. But after having made several emergency stops at speed, you will be able to halt yourself instantly on steep snow.

First of all, have your ice ax in the *correct* position before you hit the slope and start sliding out of control. You *must* have the pick part of the ice ax pointing *downward* at all times. The exception is when you are walking up or across a snow slope holding the ax like a walking stick, with one hand gripping the top of the pick. In this case, the pick must then point behind you and never forward. The reason is quite clear, if you think about it. Supposing you suddenly slip—the snow collapses beneath you, say, and rolls you downhill in a minor avalanche—then, if you just grab the bottom end of the ice ax with your other hand the ax is held across your body with the pick automatically pointing down: the proper quick arrest position instantly.

Try it now. As you slide downhill, having rolled onto your chest, in the same movement grasp the shaft of the ice ax tightly with one fist while the other grasps the head of the ax and presses the ice ax pick into the snow. The weight of your chest (and body therefore) should be pressing down on the shaft more or less right above the pick; and your hands will hold the ice ax firmly in place beneath your body. The combination of your weight pressing down and the pick jabbing into the snow will stop you surprisingly quickly. In fact, it can be so quick that the ice ax is wrenched out of your hands. This must not happen. Never drop your ice ax. It should become an instinctive reaction to hang on to it at all times on steep snow; and it is by doing these self-arrest tests over and over again that hanging on to your ice ax becomes a habit which you never lose. So, try braking to a stop from different positions. Have a friend push you down the slope as you lie headfirst on its brink; then, as you take the plunge upside down, get your feet below you and pointing downhill, and stick the ax into the slope. Of course, you will need to hold the ice ax across your chest in the right position before your partner does give you that final push, but even then it is so easy to become disoriented as you struggle to turn yourself in a feet-front position during the swift descent that you will not find it easy. That is why practicing is worth it.

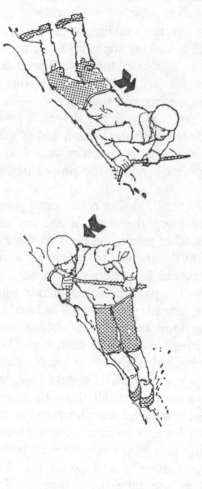

Slide downhill headfirst holding "pick" clear of snow until you have gathered up speed, then apply the end of the pick into the snow gradually. As the pick begins to bite, let the legs and body swing round until the legs are pointing downhill. Start to bring down your whole weight on the pick to drive it into the snow—and roll over until you are lying flat on the snow. The lower fist must be lowered to the snow. (Here it is shown on its way down, as the falling youth had only just begun to roll over.)

Breaking a fall down a snow slope

CLIMBING A SLIPPERY ROPE

Any rope seems slippery if you are weak in the arms and find rope climbing difficult. And it does not matter how good a gymnast you are if, one day, you need to shin up a climbing rope or some other lifeline that is nowhere near as thick and substantial as the ropes in a gymnasium which give a good grip. It is like climbing a greased pole. Yet, in a survival situation, you may have to.

However, there is a way in which you can climb up a rope and you never know when it will come in useful. The system is based on the prusik knot which can be pushed along a rope when there is nothing pulling on it, but which will lock solid when a sudden weight is applied to it. The illustration shows how, with three short rope loops all tied with prusik

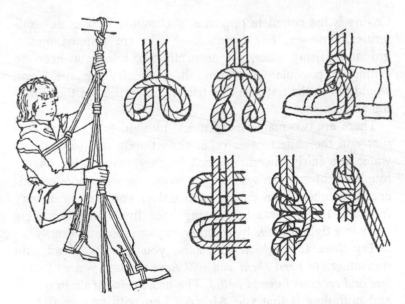

Climbing a rope with prusik-knotted loops

(*Loops must be of thinner cord or rope than the main rope*)

knots to a rope hanging from a tree branch, you can climb up that dangling rope. A word of warning, though: you can use any *sound* ropes for back yard practice, but you must never try this out on rock faces or anywhere else where the height is more than a few feet from the ground other than with proper nylon climbing rope and close supervision from experienced climbers.

One quick hint. It is much easier to practice prusiking when you weight the rope so it is under tension. Fill a rucksack or bag with rocks and tie it, just clearing the ground, to your rope. Try prusiking now. The loops can be slid up the taut rope so much easier. And you don't spin around so fast and make yourself dizzy.

CAVING

Caving is the complete opposite to climbing. There are similarities, however. For instance, if you are trapped underground by rising water, you must climb to a ledge as near the ceiling as possible (presuming it is a lofty passage); you would put to the test all those tricks you learned in the climbing experiments.

There are two main emergencies, though, that happen regularly in the easiest caves other than floodwater (and floodwater is a fairly uncommon risk in easy caves, while in the tougher subterranean systems you would be with more experienced members of a caving club unless you had been very foolhardy). The risks are: losing your lights and becoming stuck in a tight passage by trying to explore too ambitiously.

Try these tests which will stand you in good stead. But remember: *to need them you will have proved yourself careless and reckless beyond belief.* The basic safety rule in caving and potholing is that you ALWAYS go with an experienced party—usually members of a speleological club.

Experiment in a dark room with these forms of emergency lighting when your candles are finished and your batteries exhausted (or bulbs broken).

Let the eyes get used to the darkness. You will then be able to see any stray rays of light, for example, in a cave where the entrance may be only around one more corner. In a darkened room, you will soon discern where the lights shine through cracks.

Fire off a camera flashbulb (you might have one or two spare in caving kit) and then see how long the image of the room remained on the retina of your eye. Commit it to memory so that you can move quickly from A through the darkness across to B. Look especially down at the floor—in a cave this would reveal holes and steps ahead, or possibly deep water.

Use a minimum of matches (the same number, for instance that you would have in your fountain pen survival kit). Light them one by one, each time burning a piece of old clothing. Experiment which cloths burn best; certainly *not* sweaters that have become damp through the moisture in a cave. Light the bottom of the cloth as you hold it from your fingers. When it is burning too fast, lift the burning end high with a piece of stone to slow down its progress, and lengthen its illumination.

Wind scraps of paper into tight scrolls as thick as strong fence wire. You can begin best by wetting thumb and forefinger and rolling them backward and forward over one corner of the paper. Then roll it very tightly and slantwise. Light with a match and see how long it burns. Were you in a real caving situation, any paper would do —paper money, even.

GETTING OUT OF A TIGHT SQUEEZE

Imagine how it feels when you squirm headfirst beneath a low bed, pinned to the carpet. That is how it feels to be trapped crawling in a crushingly tight cave. Ask your friend to make a line of shirts, belts, whatever—and to tie a loop at one end. Then have him—remember, you are supposedly trapped and cannot move—put one of your feet in the loop. You now bend that leg and your partner secures the far end of the line tight. Straighten your leg in the loop; you will be able to inch forward. Repeat the procedure. Bend the leg. Again, the line is secured taut. Again, you straighten the leg and under the power of its muscles your body is pushed forward. Let the helpers keep on taking in the slack after you have straightened your leg, and this way you can come through a most narrow cleft relaxed—the only way to free oneself. A tense body shaking with fear will also stick fast. The quicker this rescue is performed the better, too—a body soon swells with fear and makes extrication impossible. Pulling your way through with your arms alone, incidentally, is likely to make your body swell up because it becomes too tense around the arms, shoulders, and chest under the strain of *pulling*. Push with the legs and you will soon squirm from beneath the bed.

AVOIDING BEING BURIED ALIVE

Young people venture into caves voluntarily. Picture being pulled, sucked, or hurled underground *against* your will, however. This is what happens when quicksand or an avalanche claims you. You have to act *QUICKLY*.

Try out the right survival motions in small sand dunes, gravel heaps, sawdust piles, or soft snowdrifts—anything in fact which simulates swamp so that it lets your body sink. The real risk will come on tidal flats, marshes, fens, swamps, bogs, and moorland where clumps of pale but bright green grass and reeds grow. Whenever you see tufts growing far apart in such areas—DANGER!

So you are sinking up to your knees (and beyond). Never try to keep upright. As you pull one sucked-under leg free, the other will slip down deeper, like a drowning victim. Instead, present as much body surface as possible to the quagmire. Sinking to your knees, then spreading your coat beneath you helps. So would slipping your rucksack under you.

FAST ACTION—throw yourself down flat on your face or back when you feel your legs sinking. Start swimming. Roll and twist the body in order to kick the feet clear—and keep doing this until your feet DO free themselves. Then swim the crawl or float-and-swim (depending which way up you are) to solid ground. Naturally you would fling off your rucksack or packframe at once, and try to get it beneath you. Do NOT panic. Swimming and crawling from swamps have been done many times in the past by survivors. Do NOT panic or struggle—the reason quicksands have claimed so many victims. The *more* you move, the quicker you sink.

Next, avalanches. Avoid new snow, or wind-crusted snow, lying on hard, old snow slopes, especially in hillside gullies, and you will avoid becoming an avalanche victim.

This is all right in theory, but still there is always risk. You might be a skier traversing, a walker heading for a col, or a climber tackling a steep gully, and an avalanche could strike without warning and bury you within seconds, unless you are very lucky. Furthermore, avalanches are more prevalent in many countries than ever thought possible a few years ago.

So, what do you do? It is always better to try and do something rather than nothing. Even a little action on your part could be the deciding factor in saving your life, particularly when you remember the number of avalanche survivors who have been buried alive and found in time.

Can you breathe under snow? Yes, if you end up in the avalanche tip among boulders. But avalanche survival begins seconds before you are buried. First, be suspicious of all avalanche-prone slopes. Try to avalanche them from a distance by throwing rocks. If they seem stable, then calculate your best escape route for a fast dash to safety if things start to slide.

Before starting, loosen ski bindings, and take your wrists from the loops on the ski sticks or an ice ax. These must all be jettisoned if an avalanche is triggered.

If you can hang on to an island of rocks, do so. The more snow that rushes down first, the less to bury you later. But once sliding, try to swim with a double-action backstroke. Your head will be uphill and your back will be turned to the rush of the falling mountainside. This way you can toboggan downhill rather than being submerged on the descent.

Since avalanche victims have drowned with melted snow in their lungs, keep your mouth shut tight. And, holding up a hand in front of the face to make air space, reserve your greatest effort for the end should you be buried. Then, try to break outward and upward through the snow. This must be really vigorous; the avalanche sets like concrete when it stops sliding, and you will be entombed.

If the worst happens, try your hardest NOT to panic since this shortens your survival time. You use up more oxygen for one thing. For another, it is unnecessary—search parties can locate survival victims very quickly these days with dogs.

HIGH WINDS SURVIVAL

Freak winds happen frequently on mountains. The most vulnerable areas are along actual skylines—especially where gullies run down the flanks of the peak beneath—and on rock faces.

When wind snatches at you, flatten yourself. Present as small a target of yourself to any gale as possible. Press against the rock if climbing, and wait. Fling yourself on the flat ground when walking. Before this has happened, watch your clothing. A cagoule (a long parka—with cowl—which reaches to the knees) filled with an updraft of fast-rising air can hurl you for yards and dump you over the edge.

Push all upper clothing inside the waistband of your trousers when the weather indicates gale-force winds. Always carry an ice ax (or improvised one) when walking above snow slopes even though on snow-free terrain, since there is a chance you could be blown down onto the icy surface.

MAKE A PAIR OF BAT WINGS

This experiment experiences you in feeling the power of the wind. You need a hard-frozen pond on which you can skate or slide in shoes.

Lay a piece of old blanket or sheet on the floor and tack it down. Spread yourself out on the cloth with arms extended at right angles to the body, feet spread out apart.

Ask someone to mark the cloth at the points where your wrists, ankles, and the crown of your head come. Take a felt-tipped pen and join these points with lines and, allowing for the hem, cut the bat wings from this pattern. Turn the edges over and make a strong hem all around the sail, sew in straps or bands for the ankles, waist, wrists, and head (around the brow), and that is it.

Put your bat wings on by the side of the pond. Adjust the headband around your forehead, fasten the waist, wrist, and ankle straps, and your flying machine is rigged. By spreading the arms, the wings are set. Fold the arms and the wings are furled.

Even a slight wind will speed you across the ice, especially on skates; you really feel its power. If your arms become tired from holding them out to the side, carry two long sticks which will prop them up more easily.

Bat wings on thick ice

SUPERNATURAL FEARS

KNOW it is all in the mind whenever you feel uneasy because of ghostly occurrences outdoors. There is *always* some explanation, even if it is not straightforward, yet even hardened explorers and pioneers have taken to their heels from time to time because they were *surprised* by such phenomena. It all happens so fast.

Three expert climbers saw this haunting view during an autumn evening on a 2,700-foot peak. At the summit the sky was on fire. It flamed red and yellow. Below, a sea of clouds swamped everything except jagged mountaintops. Flickering lights played around one of these. Then an enormous figure approached, but in different ways. One climber saw it beckon, another saw it shake a fist, and the third watched it stretch out both arms. A collection of mountain phenomena was what they had been watching.

The *flaming sky* was the aurora borealis or northern lights, caused by high-speed particles from the sun which are attracted to the earth's magnetic poles.

The *sea of clouds* was a temperature inversion, caused when warm air rises and the cold night air sinks into the valleys.

The *flickering lights* were probably jack-o'-lanterns or will-o'-the-wisps: spontaneous ignition of gases from rotting vegetation or perhaps a dead sheep.

The *enormous figure* was each man's Brocken specter, which was why each saw it move differently. This is when a climber suddenly sees an image of himself—apparently wearing a halo. The sun is shining through the droplets of mist—each of which forms a tiny mirror, causing the ghostly specter to appear. Airline pilots also know this phenomenon—it sometimes projects on to clouds the image of a plane hooped with rainbows.

Put down irrational fears QUICKLY in wild land. The imagination can boggle all too quickly. It IS all in the mind.

ANIMAL DANGERS

Act *FAST* when threatened by wild or tame animal life outdoors. Human reaction, when faced with danger in this way, is invariably all too slow—*you must remember what to do.* Also, you may well be carrying a rucksack, climbing rope, or other outdoor equipment when attacked, and these will hamper your escape. An attack, furthermore, can take place in the fields you are crossing en route for distant skylines. It can take you totally by surprise.

BEE STINGS

Keep your mouth shut, as a bee sting at the back of the throat can choke you to death, and gasping with fright could suck an attacker in.

Do not panic. You are far less likely to be stung if you keep calm and move slowly. Wasps, especially, sting when you panic them and, again, they could kill if they hit on a blood vessel or back of the throat. Swatting at bees and wasps is the best way to encourage an attack.

Never squeeze a bee sting. (Wasps don't leave their sting behind.) If the sting has been left in the wound, squeezing may simply force more poison into the skin. It should be eased out with a sterile needle. (Heat the point in a match, lighter, or candle flame.) Or follow the instructions in this experiment. . . .

Extract a bee sting

Wait until you have accidentally run a thorn or wooden splinter into your finger (a tiny wooden sliver is like a bee sting). Fill a narrow-mouthed bottle with hot water and pour the water out. Immediately press the bottle neck over the splinter. As the bottle cools, a partial vacuum is created and the suction will draw the splinter (or a bee sting) out quickly and cleanly.

If a stung person chokes or faints, get medical help quickly. A back-of-the-mouth sting may need an emergency operation. A blood-vessel sting can affect the heart.

SNAKES

Snake bites are rare in many countries. Be ready for such an emergency among thick grass and ferns where snakes sun themselves—and you happen to surprise one by treading on it accidentally. Remember—snakes are like fish. They will sheer away from you if you make plenty of noise and give due warning of your approach.

If a poisonous snake bites you and the venom is injected, the area will swell almost immediately. If there is no swelling, however, you have probably just been bitten and not poisoned. Frightened as you may be—and possibly only semiconscious—do not panic. Seek medical help at once by sending friends for help, or by signaling for help. (See chapter 7.) You must try to move as little as possible. The more you move your limbs, the faster the poison will spread and reach your heart. Wipe—NOT rub—the bitten area with a handkerchief. It is better not to lance it or try to suck out the poison.

It can help to apply a firm bandage on the heart side of the bite. Loosen it for one minute every half hour. It also helps if you have killed the snake and can take it to the doctor with you.

DOGS

Any dog is mad who is rushing for you, jaws snapping—only mad with rage possibly, but still mad. Do not dodge or run. Stand still! Additionally, a shouted "GO AWAY" may just turn the tide in your favor.

When the dog has not left and IS attacking, remain standing (you are completely at a savage dog's mercy once on the ground); punch it on the nose; offer an arm for it to grab so that it will leave the rest of you alone; be prepared to kick it in the throat if you can keep your balance and are swift-footed; throw a jacket, cagoule, anorak, duvet, or lifejacket (whatever you are carrying) over its head to blind it; try to grab it by the scruff of the neck as *quickly* as possible, but skip clutching for its tail or it will spin round and bite you. If the dog is gripping your arm between its teeth on no account try to rip your arm away, or you will have a torn wound instead of a clean bite—it is better to push the limb toward the back of the attacker's throat and, if you have pushed hard enough, the dog may let go. Talk to the dog quietly, too, while it is gripping you.

NEVER touch a strange dog. And, when bitten, wash the bite under running cold water. Wash in soap and water. (Do not rub.) See a doctor quickly for an antirabies injection.

HORSES AND COWS

Watch out in high winds. Horses become noticeably upset in big gusts; they hate the wind in their ears. They become uneasy and jittery. Approaching thunderstorms and lightning will also make horses a threat. Avoid the centers of fields, or the whole fields themselves if possible, where there are horses. And never turn your back on them.

In the countryside cows can be more dangerous than bulls, because you don't expect trouble. They are unpredictable, however. Thunder in the air, lightning, or high winds can make them charge. Many people have been killed because, unlike a bull, a cow does not look dangerous. Survival depends on throwing away whatever you happen to be carrying as you run, or strip off your clothing and throw it piece by piece as you sprint for the wall. The animal—and a bull will do the same too—will be temporarily distracted by them, leaving you to run for safety.

SWANS

These large birds can break an adult's arm with one blow from a wing. Dogs make them violent. They are also very sensitive when they have cygnets with them. To drive off an angry swan, lightly splash it with water.

6

SURVIVAL JOURNEY
ON WATER

SPEED is also a key factor in taking correct survival action
in water. It may be to escape from a burning cabin cruiser, or
to catch up with your capsized small dinghy which is racing
away with the tide. You may even have shot a sluice uninten-
tionally and now, in the frothing water which is roaring like
an angry beast, you face drowning.

FIRST, THERE IS NO EXCUSE FOR NOT BEING
ABLE TO SWIM. IT REALLY IS THE VITAL FAC-
TOR IN AQUATIC SURVIVAL. EVERY SURVIVAL
SITUATION THAT IS THREATENED BY DROWN-
ING MEANS THE NONSWIMMER IS GOING TO
HAVE A DREADFUL STRUGGLE: WITHOUT THIS
SO NECESSARY SKILL YOU CANNOT GUARAN-
TEE SUCCESS—NO MATTER HOW HARD YOU
TRY TO IMPROVISE. SUCH MAKESHIFT METH-
ODS OF FLOATING DO WORK SOMETIMES, OF
COURSE, BUT YOU CANNOT BANK ON THEM IN
THE SAME WAY THAT THE COMPETENT SWIM-
MER CAN. THIS, IN FACT, IS A SURVIVAL SITUA-
TION WHERE THE NONSWIMMER WILL BE IN-
DEED LUCKY TO KEEP BREATHING.

There is one technique that swimmers and nonswimmers alike ought to practice—how to get into a circular life preserver in the shallow end of the pool (should you ever need to do this as you are struggling in deep water). It is NOT easy.

Grip the nearest part of the life preserver with both hands on top, knuckles up. Pull it close to your chin, and avoid panic—*for the moment, you are floating and have grabbed support.* Now, pull the edge of the life preserver beneath the water, at the same time flipping it vertically up in the air so it

Getting into a life preserver

sticks out of the water. Push the *bottom* edge away from you so that the life preserver now begins to fall over your head. Wriggle head and shoulders up through it as it drops down over your body. Bring your arms up through and over in much the same movement.

Another basic technique that should be familiar to swimmer and nonswimmer is floating. The natural buoyancy in your body will keep you floating on the surface of water as long as you relax. Although you can float on your back or face down, try it lying back, as if in bed and looking at the ceiling. First, draw in a deep breath, then *stick your chin upward and press the back of your head into the water.* Keep breathing and keep your body quite limp. Allow the legs and feet to rise to their own level in the water; as long as your face just clears the surface of the water you can float all day. For this experiment it is essential to have the co-operation of someone who will initially hold your head (and probably the rest of you) until you feel confident enough to relax and successfully float.

Relaxed, vertical swimming in one spot, using the minimum amount of energy to keep your head above water—which is what treading water is all about—is one of the most important survival skills. As with floating on your back, you should try, try, and try again until you can do it without a second thought.

The best place to try is in that part of the pool where the water laps against your eyebrows when you stand on the bottom. Stand near the side, too, for extra confidence. Now begin the movements which will support you in an upright position, freewheeling in water. Begin to pedal your feet as if on a bicycle and hold the hands out so they can describe wide circling movements just beneath the surface of the water. As both feet and hands press down, aim to keep your nose and mouth clear of the water. Maintain calm, regular breathing *and* a slow relaxed kick. You will find it much easier to do than it sounds if, on the whole, you are nervous of water. It will encourage you if you see a dog taken to deep water for the first time. By holding its chin for a few seconds it then instinctively knows how to tread water, and what a dog can do you ought to be able to do. But you will need a companion to get you started.

DROWNPROOFING

Can you dip your face into a sink full of warm water at home, open your eyes, relax completely, and like it? Yes? Then, you are well on the way to being able to drownproof yourself in deep water—a method which will keep you buoyant effortlessly in the worst conditions. If you do not like immersing your face, however, then you should count this washbasin trial as the first experiment and persevere with ducking your head below the surface until you can peer at the basin plug in comfort. While doing this, also practice building up air pressure in your nose to prevent getting water up your nostrils. You can do this by seeming to blow through the nose without expelling any air. Try this nonblow blowing—it really works.

Drownproofing is a more effective way of staying put in one place in water than merely treading water (this means you are holding your head out of water—a weight of between 10–15 pounds—which eventually becomes tiring), or floating. (Choppy water will make it impossible for you to keep waves from swilling down your nostrils and mouth.) The survivor who drownproofs himself copies wildlife like the alligator or seal who can float for hours with their heads below water—just taking an occasional breath now and then. It is the most efficient method of using natural buoyancy too.

Fill your lungs with air and drop into the water so that you are entirely immersed. Keep your mouth closed tight and your eyes open. Then you can watch for the moment when the light shows, which means your head is just about to break the surface of the water. Relax and spread eagle your arms forward loosely, legs hanging down so that your trunk swings to the horizontal position. And try to keep your face under.

Hold your breath for several seconds, then prepare to take a new one. Press your lips together, but snort out air through the nostrils. Then start to lift the head upward and backward as you stroke down in the water with the palms of both hands. As your mouth clears the surface, breathe in quietly and dip your face back into the water again. Incidentally, do not lift your head high and in a hurry. *The fact that your head completely clears the water means that its weight (10–15 pounds, remember) presses your body down farther into the water* which could make you panic. It is when you are completely submerged, just the back of the head showing above the surface, that you are most buoyant. So forget about fighting to keep your head above water; that will be the very reason you sink.

This is an important principle to remember in certain survival situations . . . the fact that whenever you raise a limb or any part of the body clear of the surface of the water, then

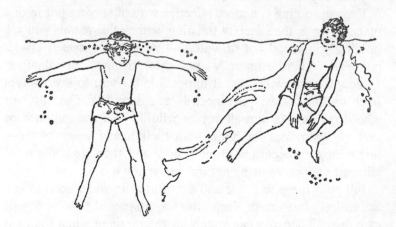

Drownproofing

that part of you immediately becomes much heavier than the comparative weightlessness of the rest of your submerged body. And so it presses you down deeper below the surface. In fact, it is the major factor in saving your skin when you need to sink like a stone. There are such occasions.

Finally, let us look at a way of survival swimming whereby you can make yourself all the more buoyant by using the very clothes you happen to be wearing when you are thrown into deep water. Do not consider these methods as short cuts to safety. You still need to be able to swim—and to swim well enough to be confident in water. It is just that these extra floating methods will give you an even greater margin of buoyancy and, therefore, greater ability and encouragement to keep hanging on.

MAKE A LIFE JACKET FROM PAJAMAS

Your clothing, once you have rid yourself of shoes and heavy garments, can be made into bags of air which will ride you high in the water with no effort at all. Try these experiments first of all in your bath at home, then carry them out in a swimming pool while treading water.

Fill your bath with warm water and climb in wearing pajamas. First, take off the trousers underwater so that you get the feel of having to drag wet cloth over your limbs, and then, the jacket. (It should be buttoned up.) The correct way is to pull it from the bottom up to your armpits, then reach behind you and ruck it all up in both hands at the nape of your neck. Now yank it over the top of your head, and clear of your face, in one fast wriggle. Practice this so that you never make the mistake of dragging the wet pajama top onto your face—it could stop your breathing.

Lie back in the bath after fastening the collar of the

pajama top the wrong way around your neck. Button it
at the back. Then knot the cuffs of both sleeves. The garment is now hanging down the front of your body like a
bib. Lie well back so the water comes to your chin, as if
you were floating in the sea, and flap the garment with an
up through the air and down movement so that the bottom of the pajamas is finally held below the surface of the
water in front of your stomach. The air that is trapped
(as a result of the flapping) in the sleeves and the body
of the pajamas will balloon up considerably—and there
is your life jacket. Do keep a firm hold on the bottom of
the garment still under water though, or air will escape.
If it does (and inflated clothing will be leaking air all the
time), keep topping it up either by swinging it through
the air again, blowing air directly through the wet fabric
from the outside with your mouth, or by scooping air up
into the bottom opening with a hand.

Trousers can also be filled with air. Knot each trouser leg
at the cuffs and secure buttons and zippers. Hold the
empty trousers behind your head like a coal sack while
sitting in the bath. Suddenly swirl them over your head so
they balloon with air and plunge the waistband of the
trousers beneath the level of the water to trap this air inside.

Stick your head between the inflated legs of your pajamas, the back of the neck resting in the crotch. Now
you can float on your back as you grip the bottom ends
of each leg in front of you—trapping the air. You have
now made the horseshoe type of life preserver.

Although space will be restricted in your bathroom, you
will be able to get a good idea of how the clothing does fill
like sausages with air. It is when trying out these tactics while
treading water in the deep end of a swimming pool, however,

that you will really learn their value for they really do buoy you up.

Making clothes into a life jacket

CAPSIZAL SURVIVAL EXPERIMENTS

Find a river pool where local people swim—in other words, a *safe* place. A private pool will also do. Public swimming pools are no good for the simple reason that you are now going to experiment with various forms of objects in water, boats for instance.

Try by trial and error—whether you can or cannot swim—those types of objects which float in water, and which you can hang on to if you find them in the water with you by accident, design, or because someone has thrown something to you so that you can hang on until help comes.

Certain hats will float when pressed down on water, so will Wellington boots, rucksacks full AND empty (try both ways), buckets, table-tennis balls stuffed in pockets, footballs stuffed up a sweater, old plastic detergent bottles. Sponges are NOT buoyant nor are many spare wheels of cars. Plastic bags inflated will float, so do planks, so do car seats, AND do try crates, barrels, boxes, driftwood, oil drums, rubber tires, and a quick-blow-up air mattress that is still partially empty.

CAPSIZAL RULES

The right order of actions after capsizing in a canoe or small boat in deep water is the same. Whatever type of boat you have, whether canoe, small dinghy, or rubber raft, take it into the deepest part of your safe water, capsize it, and carry out the following drill . . .

Stay with the craft (even if it is, in the real-life crunch, being swept out to sea). The boat gives you something to cling to, and can be seen more easily by people who can help. Try swimming alone in a strong current running out to sea, and it is most unlikely you would reach the beach.

Collect the most important buoyant items—oars, paddles, floats, etc., *but do not let your craft slip away when a driving wind or current is pulling at it.*

Go to one end of the boat and hang on. Try this one too —swim under the capsized shell when it is a roomy hull (like a row boat) and come up inside. Hold on to the seats and breathe the air trapped inside the boat. You would do this in a real-life-situation storm if, at sea, you found yourself unable to cling to, or climb on top of, a slippery hull. You would then be able to re-emerge when the water became calmer.

Fully inflate your life jacket—if you are wearing this kind.

Collect other floating gear if you can do it safely and easily.

Tie yourself to the boat. If there is any chance of your being in the water for some time, use any short line before your fingers become too stiff to tie knots. You must never let the boat slip away. And it can.

Devise ways of making yourself conspicuous. A swimmer and capsized boat are very low in the water and even in moderate waves may be out of sight in wave troughs for 80 per cent of the time. Attach any bright-colored clothing (orange, red, and fluorescent materials are best) to an oar or paddle and hold it in a vertical position like a flagpole. A colored flag even only 3 ft. or 4 ft. (1 m.) above water level enormously increases the possibility of being seen from a search boat or the shore. (See chapter 7.)

SWIM A CANOE TO THE BANK

Grasp the upstream end of a capsized canoe, do a flutter kick and head directly for the riverbank. This experiment is even more authentic if there is a current carrying you downstream at the same time. Eventually you will reach the side, although the current will have taken you well downstream too.

> WARNING: Make sure before any experiment there is no sluice or rapids below your stretch of "safe" water. You could possibly be swept on toward a hazard accidentally.

WHIRLPOOL SURVIVAL

Go to your nearest sluice; this will have similar undercurrents to the vortex of a whirlpool. Take two or three empty plastic detergent bottles which you have painted red, yellow, and bright blue. Fill the red bottle half full of water so that the bottle will float below the surface of the water. Fill the yellow

Swimming down in a sluice

bottle almost full of water so that it sinks slowly. And leave the blue bottle full of air. Stopper them all, and toss them into the center of froth below the waterfall. (This is the place YOU would surface if you had been sucked over the sill of the sluice). Watch the bottles. The blue one will stay trapped on the surface of white water. The red and yellow bottles will disappear. One or both, however, *will* emerge lower down the river . . . showing you the right action to take *if you are ever caught in this crisis.*

You would swim DOWN for the riverbed. The undercurrents would then carry you safely downstream under water and eject you past the danger point. Keep trying to swim on the surface of the white water, however, and you will get nowhere—just exhausted with your failing efforts. If you are holding on to a capsized boat in this position . . . abandon the boat. You will probably lose this and all your gear, but you will save your life. *Throwing plastic bottles into rivers pollutes the water. Collect the bottles afterward by throwing stones and driving them to the side where you can retrieve them and take them home or tie them to strings.*

HOLE IN THE ICE

Pretend you are crossing an iced-up river when suddenly, and without a moment's warning, the frosted sheet covering the water caves in. You can simulate this horrific situation in a swimming pool or a safe bathing spot in a local river.

Place on the water anything solid that floats. It could be an inflated car tire inner tube, a blown-up air mattress, a home-made raft made from planks and oil drums or a tiny dinghy. Whatever it is, it represents the ice. Stand astride it wearing trousers and shirt, and push off from the side with a long pole or branch which will help you keep your balance as you wobble upright out into the middle of the water. Now, deliberately upset your "ice floe" once you are well clear of the side of the water. As it tilts and you take the plunge:

GIVE A BIG KICK (BREAST-STROKE LEG ACTION).

SPRAWL WITH YOUR ARMS ACROSS THE PIECE OF "ICE."

CONTINUE KICKING WITH THE LEGS AND TRY TO CRAWL BACK ON TOP.

That first big kick was an effort to jump up out of the water with the top half of your clothing still dry. Then, you must head immediately for the remaining unbroken ice which will give you a chance to save yourself before a strong current sweeps you away underneath it (in this case, your raft or whatever). By kicking hard with the feet and reaching out with your arms across it, you should be able to wriggle back on top.

Reaching out for sound ice

Of course, the strong current mentioned above is only imaginary, the kind of thing that could face you in a *real* survival situation. During your survival training, however, you should stick to calm waters which are completely free from hazards as mentioned before. Fooling about with air mattresses, inner tubes, or makeshift rafts on water running with strong currents is obviously dangerous, and you should keep well away from them. This applies to both rivers and the sea.

The fact that the water is calm does not make the experiment worthless. It will still give you a good idea of how to deal with collapsed ice in a true-life situation. Incidentally, if this were the real thing and if you were carrying a sheath knife, stab this into the ice as far as you can reach and hang on to it. In really cold weather your sleeves will freeze to the ice, meaning some extra purchase. Even thin ice can support you as long as you keep kicking in the water; this gives you the chance to reach stronger ice which will support your weight.

Never go on new ice before making sure it is strong enough. Ice is rarely the same thickness throughout. For instance, it's usually stronger close to land. New ice melts under sunshine. And wind also affects thickness of ice. (It creates waves underneath which weaken the surface in ripples.) Finally, if a ladder is pushed out to you by rescuers, grasp the nearest rung, heave yourself up out of the water, and drag yourself along until you are lying full length along the ladder and can be slid to safety by the helpers.

DEALING WITH A HOSTILE CURRENT

Choose a smooth stretch of river which has a *fairly* strong current, but no hazards (like sluice, rocks, or rapids). It is also important that you are a competent swimmer. Practice swimming diagonally against the current starting from one side and finishing upstream on the other bank.

Also try to battle against the river's current *direct;* you will discover that this is much more strenuous work, but at least it will teach you to swim diagonally across powerful currents or riptides which could trap you near a beach. Always swim *across* them, and never *against*. This way you can reach safety before you become absolutely exhausted. But don't try this at sea where there is a risk you really may be swept out. A safe stretch of clear *river* water is the best trial ground—with safe, easy angled banks on either side.

7

WAYS AND MEANS OF
CALLING FOR HELP

HOW do you attract attention so that the people observing
your signals know you really do want help? For example, a
train engineer may be just about to pass through a long tunnel, when on a nearby hillside he sees a group of young people
waving at him. Well, everyone waves at engineers. He will
probably wave right back, and in seconds be gone. Yet, that
party of youngsters might have been in desperate straits,
perhaps out hiking in rough country and one of them has just
been bitten by a deadly snake. Still some way from the railway
tracks, they had waved in the hope that the engineer might
discern their plight and stop. But not much hope there, I am
afraid, and quite understandably so.

And then again, with what do we signal when a crisis is
upon us? Things seem to happen so quickly, everything ap-
pears much worse than it probably is, and you feel it is the
end of the world. Thinking about the right sequence of dots
and dashes by which to send a Morse message, or how to per-
form the right arm actions with which to semaphore a pilot
overhead, are the last things we consider as blood spurts,
bones break, and we are fighting to catch our breath in foam-
ing water. Yet, if assistance is within reasonable distance, we
must drive our thoughts toward reaching it.

Calling "HELP!" is not always as difficult as you may think, however. In fact, many young people have found help when they were in a desperate plight stuck high up a rock face and struck by lightning, or marooned on an islet in mid-river with their raft wrecked and the river rising fast in torrential rainfall. At times like this, you must act fast. Furthermore, you must get the meaning of your signals over. If you really do need to signal a train, for example, because you know there is a tree lying across the tracks just ahead and around a bend, then you need to know the recognized way of flagging down the engineer by using the signal he will understand. It is no use just waving. Your actions have to *mean* something.

It follows from this that it pays to know the different *ways* of signaling help. There are more than you may think, and many of them can be improvised from items carried on you, or which you find nearby.

Now, you might think that waving a white handkerchief is a pretty tame kind of signal. Yet, it is the one distress signal which can make you stand out in a crowd of a hundred thousand people. The occasion here is at a giant stadium where an important football game is being played and a friend has fainted in the swaying, cheering crowd. But, if you wave a white handkerchief—and get those spectators around you to wave their handkerchiefs and programs too—that signal means "HELP!" to the ambulance and first-aid men down by the sidelines on the pitch. They will come to the rescue— simply because a group of people waving anything white has its own special meaning for *them*.

It is great fun carrying out signaling experiments with a friend across a stretch of open countryside, but not just yet. Let us first look at the people who are most likely to receive your distress signal, and the types of signal which mean something to them. For obvious reasons, avoid trying out such signals in actual practice where they could be interpreted wrongly and result in a false alarm. An instance of this would be your sending up a distress rocket from a small boat when, in fact, you were all right and were just interested in seeing what the rocket looked like in action. . . . And the local lifeboat was launched.

Here, then, is your list of potential rescuers and how you can make your meaning clear to them.

Train engineers

Only in the direst circumstances would you stop a train. But, when such a situation arises, stand by the tracks facing the on-coming locomotive. Raise both arms above your head. A train can be stopped at night by swinging a light from side to side as you stand by the tracks facing toward the driver.

Motorists and truck drivers

Signal that your car or truck has broken down by raising both the lid of the hood and the trunk. Tie a white rag or handker-chief to the radio aerial. Switch on the near-side flasher when the car you have been traveling in is stuck in a dangerous position. Take off a hubcap, and place it on the road about 50 yards (45 m.) from the rear of the car to warn approaching traffic by setting fire to oily rags inside this dish.

Any form of red triangle—constructed from bits and pieces if you are not carrying a proper safety signal of this type—should also be propped up on the road to give warning well in advance of the obstacle.

You do not have a car? And have, in fact, only just stum-bled on the road because it passes through wild country and you are going to fetch help for a friend who is lying out there injured? Remember that some highways have emergency tele-phones at regular intervals. As to the best way to stop traffic that is speeding past: improvise a notice which says "HELP! —POLICE" or "HELP!—AMBULANCE."

Forest workers

Smoke is an instant warning to a lumberjack. Fire watches are kept on all big stretches of woodland in dry weather. Be careful when fire-lighting, however, should you ever be castaway in a deserted forest, as trees can blaze when sparks go astray from your fire. *Extreme caution is vital here.*

Farmers

Shouts, whistles, lights, and makeshift flags will all attract a farmer's attention. So will throwing stones and rolling large rocks downhill. As farmers usually have keen eyesight and excellent hearing, anything out of the ordinary on their land will be noted, but you must keep signaling so that the farmer in question investigates further. In the mountains, the sight of sheep running (you threw stones at them, for example) will rivet a farmer's attention from miles away. Such would be the case if you were lying injured on a hillside with a broken leg. You spot the farmer and his dogs far below. Although you wave, he takes no notice. If you could make nearby sheep scatter, however (say, by releasing your dog which is not trained *not* to run after these animals), there is a chance your waving and shouting will have an effect—once the farmer sees part of his flock being disturbed. Such drastic action is only permissible in a serious situation. Remember that farmers are used to seeing young people hiking throughout the year and in bad weather. You need to use everything at your disposal to seize their attention. And that goes for ALL your signaling attempts no matter in what kind of countryside you may be.

Airplane and helicopter pilots

Pilots are also used to seeing people trekking across tracts of wild countryside. You need something special to attract their attention. And do not forget; the pilots of some aircraft may be flying at an altitude of over 30,000 ft. (9,000 m.) which is higher than Everest. Yet, you can still make yourself visible to a pilot so far away that you can neither see nor hear the plane.

Dazzling the pilot with regular mirror flashes from the sun is the method you must use. If there is no sun, though, you will have to resort to other signals like bonfires, signals laid out on the ground, distress rockets, or perhaps waving a flashlight into the sky. It is, then, a matter of using whatever you can. But, whenever there is sun, find something that will reflect it—even a shiny green leaf has been used with success as a mirror.

Basically, the idea is to keep flashing at the sky with a mirror until you are noticed by the pilot of an aircraft who will then fly toward the bright spot for a closer look. It is now as

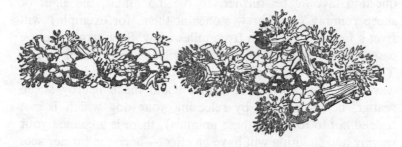

Vital ground-air signals

he zooms overhead, that you spell out your plea for assistance by already having laid out ground-to-air signals as shown. (These can be made from just about any available materials, as we shall see.)

The two most important signals are the one for "DOCTOR NEEDED" and the other for "PROCEED IN DIRECTION OF ARROW" or "AM GOING THIS WAY." You would use this last sign if you had already left the scene of a crash—a wrecked car, say—and you are making an attempt to walk to safety. The ground-to-air arrow signal would then tell a pilot the direction of your following movements.

There is another way of getting your message over to an aircraft pilot: semaphoring with your arms and legs as shown.

Smoke signals will attract low-flying aircraft, especially when a search has already been mounted for you. Obvious smoke from a bonfire could just do the trick. The most effective bonfire signal, however—and the distress signal that is universally recognized by pilots—is to have three signal bonfires laid out in an equilateral triangle. The area should have sides a hundred paces long in a clearing big enough for a light plane or helicopter to land. But, the fires should still be close enough so that you can reach and ignite all three with burning torches in twenty seconds—the time it takes an aircraft to pass overhead.

When you have absolutely nothing with which to signal other than the countryside around you, use that. Spoil it. Any trampled-flat and beaten-up-looking terrain can persuade the pilot of a search aircraft to take a closer look. And then—as we shall see—any letters spelling out "SOS" dug into snow or sand, or spelled out in letters made up from heaps of stones and earth, can prove eye-catching too. Because these large letters cast shadows, they can even be read in moonlight by an aircraft passing overhead.

Mountaineers, backpackers, and hikers

The international mountain distress signal is obvious to anyone who hears it: six whistle blasts blown in a minute, then a minute's silence, then six more blasts repeated—and so on. The reply by anyone who hears this cry for help is three whistle blasts a minute followed by a minute's silence, then the three blasts a minute repeated—and so on.

If you have no whistle, then you can use a flashlight instead. Flick the ON/OFF switch to the same sequence as

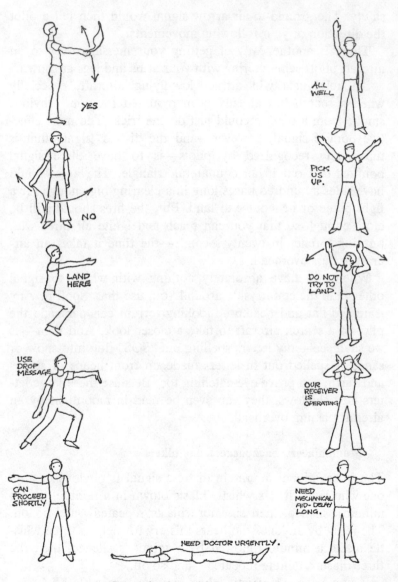

YES

ALL WELL

NO

PICK US UP.

LAND HERE

DO NOT TRY TO LAND.

USE DROP MESSAGE

OUR RECEIVER IS OPERATING

CAN PROCEED SHORTLY

NEED MECHANICAL AID- DELAY LONG.

NEED DOCTOR URGENTLY.

Semaphoring with body signals

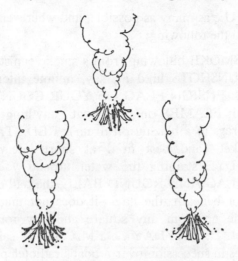

SOS beacon signals

Above is the most effective distress signal and one that is universally recognized by pilots—three bonfires set out in an equilateral triangle

described above. But only if you have a spare supply of flashlight bulbs. The reason is given later in this chapter.

The international Morse code distress signal is different; for this, you would simply blow three short whistle blasts followed by three longer blasts and ending with three short blasts again. Then you would pause. And repeat the three short, three long, and three short blasts once more (and so have spelled out "SOS" . . . "SOS" in Morse code). However, in mountain country, it is best to stick to the international mountain distress signal. The sound of any whistle's blast will make other climbers pay attention. Once they hear the six shrills a minute, then you will have their *undivided* attention.

Sailors and coast guards

There are a number of different distress signals which can be used at sea. Use as many as possible, and wherever applicable. Choose from the following:

ORANGE SMOKE billowing from a smoke canister in broad daylight; GUNSHOTS fired at, say, minute intervals; THE NATIONAL ENSIGN FLAG OF YOUR COUNTRY flying upside down; FLAMES on your boat (anything from gasoline-soaked rags to a blazing oil drum); RED STARS falling from a rocket (and best fired at short intervals); SEA MARKER DYE staining the water around your boat; A SQUARE FLAG AND ROUND BALL, the ball either being on top of, or beneath, the flag—it does not matter—which can be made up from any square and any round object; "MAYDAY . . . MAYDAY . . . MAYDAY" said—as here —three times in succession over a boat's radiotelephone (then you give the name of the boat, her position, and the crisis you are facing); . . . — — — . . . (yes, the Morse code signal previously explained) but this time signaled over a boat's radiotelegraph; RAISING BOTH ARMS OUT TO THE SIDE, then lowering them slowly, then raising them again, and so on; A RED LIGHT burning from a hand-held flare (or from a tiny parachute released by a distress rocket); "NC"—these letters flown as code flags stand for "I am in distress and need help fast" in the international code of signals; BOOMING TONES that sound repeatedly—signaling on any available boat's fog-signaling equipment.

WAYS OF SIGNALING

Before we experiment with the different methods of attracting attention, there are two important points to bear in mind. The first is that you should always be very careful when using signals which will eventually become exhausted. Signals, for example, like bonfires, rockets, and flashlights can only last so long, while waving your arms, flying flags, and blowing a whistle will last as long as you manage to survive. Therefore, only use expendable signals when there is a good chance of rescue—were this *a real* emergency—and you know that help is within reach. Otherwise you stand a chance of using up your signals with no one to see them and being left with nothing to show for your pains.

Second, *keep signaling.* Use those methods which—like a flag flying—are always on show, and have in readiness those more eye-catching signals, like an unlit bonfire which is then ready and can be ignited at the critical moment when an aircraft suddenly skims into view low over the horizon. This means you can always be trying some form of signaling. If there are two of you, say, stuck on a high mountain col, one of you can be flashing with a mirror during the hours of sunlight, while the other lays out ground-to-air signals, prepares three bonfires, possibly does some signaling, and so on.

And so to some signaling experiments you can do now. Learn how to improvise with just about any old materials. You don't need a polished stainless-steel mirror to signal an aircraft, for example. A tin-can lid with a hole punched through the middle will do fine. Always be on the lookout, therefore, for all other means of signaling help. For instance, did you know that a vertical metal pipe about 2 in. (5 cm.) in diameter and from 6 ft. to 20 ft. (2 m.–6 m.) long will sound like a foghorn if you burn paper at its base? Now, it is unlikely you will have such a metal tube when you need to signal help, but people have been saved by calling for aid in a low booming tone rather than a shrill scream, which is on the same lines; the low notes carry farther and longer than the higher-pitched ones. Well, it is this same line of thinking about a subject to which you would normally not give a second thought—i.e., signals for help—which can save you in a catastrophe. So, always be on the lookout for all the unusual ways of attracting attention you can discover during these following experiments.

WHISTLE TESTS

Walk into open countryside with a friend and separate so there are a few hundred yards between you. Now, take turns blowing different whistles, and listen to the result. These should be all kinds of whistles, varying from a toy whistle of the Christmas cracker type to the Acme Thunderer whistle as used by police forces and mountain rescue teams.

Even try to do the whistle used by shepherds. Stick two fingers in your mouth, using either the first two fingers or the first and third finger. Press them against the tip of your tongue. Blow through the gap between your fingers, and eventually you will be able to do a really shrill whistle—as long as you avoid trying to press the tongue too far back. You will be heard for miles with practice.

You can make a survival whistle too. Find a straight piece of sycamore twig six inches long. Use a knife or sharp stone to score a ring through the bark halfway along. Now wet the bark and tap it several times on a stone. This should let you twist and slide a sleeve of bark from the wood. (Spring is the easiest time to do this, incidentally, as the sap lubricates the bark.) Pare away a thin section from the top of the newly revealed wood with your knife as shown. And cut a nick in the bark.

After fitting the sleeve and the wood together again, blow through the end. No joy? Keep trying with different lengths of twig and by using different twigs from a variety of sycamores.

Another type of whistle can be cut from the stems of beaked parsley which grows in hedgebanks. Snap off a short length, and you should find the stem is hollow. Cut a nick in the tube near one end, place a finger over the other end and blow.

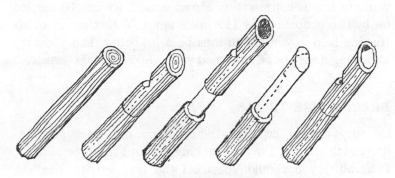

Sycamore whistle
(*Can be made from other trees*)

Wetting your whistle means drinking to ease your throat muscles, which will swell up if you yell too frantically. Always try to have water nearby—even if just a bottleful especially saved for the occasion—when you need to shout and find your voice has gone. Try this now by shouting yourself hoarse after a friend and yourself have separated in a forest or open countryside. Then, drink from a stream or a bottle of soda pop. You will find you can shout twice as hard, although previously the vocal chords had almost given up under the strain. And do shout in that low-register, deep-toned voice that is reminiscent of a foghorn as mentioned earlier in this chapter. It is more effective than a higher-pitched voice. A voice is like a flashlight battery, after all; save it until you have a chance of being heard, and then it will not have been exhausted. Incidentally, it helps to plug both ears with your fingers—you shout all the louder when you cannot hear yourself doing it.

Last of all, remember that sound travels almost a mile a second in water—four and a half times faster than in air (the speed of sound in air being about 1,100 feet per second). And voices and noise will carry to amazing distances over calm water or ice. A conversation across smooth ice can be carried on by two people nearly 1½ miles apart. Your chances of attracting help in winter can thus be a lot better than you may ever imagine as your deep-toned yells will carry even farther.

BEACON FIRE TRIALS

Be very careful, especially when there are trees and undergrowth nearby. Practice making bonfires in all conditions. Preferably, you should construct the fires in dry weather, cover them up, then try to light them on a wet and windy day, just as you would if you were a castaway on a desert isle and suddenly a ship hoves into view.

We have already seen in chapter 3 how to light a fire. Here are some extra tips concerning signal fires:

Do as you would do in a survival situation. Make three signal bonfires one hundred paces apart in a triangle formation. Cover up two of them under slates, stones, sods, foliage, and any other shelter. You would light the third fire for warmth in a real crisis, if there was plenty of fuel available, and sit between it and a large boulder or rock outcrop for extra warmth.

Treasure spare fuel. Hoard it near each bonfire or, if there is one particular place where it will keep dry best, store it here.

Practice setting light to a bonfire so that you know how to do it in rain and wind. For example, striking a match is difficult with cold fingers on a breezy day. The best way to set about it is to blow on your hands first to make them warmer (or warm both hands beneath the armpits), then face the wind and cup your hands to make a bowl. Hold the box of matches and the match in this, and, as you ignite the match, tilt its head downward into the shield of both palms so the flame runs back up the matchstick. It is also a good tip to know that damp matches can be dried by rubbing gently in your dry hair or sideburns.

Any oil- or gasoline-soaked rags are great fire-starters. Keep them handy if you have them, say, as a result of your transport being wrecked and your being left stranded. Another first-class fire-lighter is a blazing spruce torch. (Careful, *please*, if you try this in woodland.) To try this, look for such branches on the ground; do not rip them from trees when practicing.

SENDING SMOKE SIGNALS

"Smoke by day, fire by night" is a good watchword to remember when you need help. Make your own smoke from bonfires, but it is useful to know that you can buy smoke canisters from ship's chandlers; these produce orange-colored smoke which shows up well in daylight.

The smoke you make will be either black or white. Thick black smoke is ideal for overcast skies and gloomy days, as you can see if your friend lights a fire and sends up black smoke signals about a mile away. What makes black smoke? The answer is pieces of any kind of rubber, bits of plastic, oily rags, or lumps of grease on the flames. Another good substance for black smoke is expanded polystyrene, the synthetic white corklike plastic which is used in small boats to give buoyancy (as well as in packing radios, cameras, and other instruments you buy new from a shop). In fact, this material will float on water and give off heavy black smoke at the same time (useful to know when you are lost at sea in a small boat and want to send up a smoke signal without setting fire to your vessel—the burning plastic can float nearby).

How about thick white smoke, though? This shows up best on clear days with blue skies. And all you need is damp moss, green boughs, and a regular sprinkling of water (urine if necessary).

MAKE A POCKET HANDKERCHIEF DISTRESS FLIER

There are two kinds: kites and flags. The only cloth needed for a kite is a handkerchief or large square rag torn from a piece of old clothing. Lay this flat on the ground. Now, lay two thin springy twigs across the cloth diagonally from corner to corner. Secure each corner of the cloth to the end of a twig by tying with bits of string, shoelace, wire, or whatever you have handy. Also, tie the cross-over join where the two twigs meet in the middle of the cloth square. After doing this your piece of cloth should now be stretched tight, stressed by the two diagonal twigs which should be in a "bowed" away position from the cloth. Tie two short pieces of string—say, about 18 in. (45 cm.) long—near opposite ends of one of the twigs, then tie these strings to the long string by which you are going to fly your kite. Ready? Let the wind fill the kite so that it balloons out the cloth away from the twig struts and carries it up into the sky—you paying out or pulling in the string, of course.

Flags are best seen when waved slowly. Try it now as your friend stands on one hill a good distance away from your own position. But, when a flagpole is needed, use anything—stick, pole, tree trunk, rocky bluff, canoe paddle, or whatever.

There is one particularly significant test you should do if you canoe or sail a small boat. Have a friend wait on the beach. Then, canoe a good distance out to sea or onto the lake. Tie a flag—anything that looks like one will do—to a paddle or oar, raise it high and wave it backward and forward. The moving flag will flutter in its own breeze on a calm day, and it becomes so much more an obvious signal for help.

If flags need to be flown as high as possible, they should also contrast with the background. Red, yellow, or orange are fine contrasting colors. When only white cloth is available, dirty it up with soil, oil, mud, anything filthy.

SEND DAZZLING FLASHES WITH A TIN CAN LID

This is how to dazzle the pilot of a high-flying aircraft to attract his attention. But keep this experiment at ground level by flashing, instead, a friend who is standing a good distance away across rough country. Do not flash at passing planes, for obvious reasons. For one thing, you could momentarily blind the pilot of a low-altitude aircraft if your sun-and-mirror flash caught him unawares. For another, the pilot may think you really are in trouble and there could be serious consequences.

Punch a hole through the middle of the can lid. This should have two bright and shiny sides which you can now polish even brighter with the cuff of your sleeve. It is the only equipment you need.

The next thing is to estimate the position of the sun and your friend (who is going to pick up your signal if it is successful). Say the angle of the sun and his position is less than 90°. Then go about signaling him this way:

Method A

Hold the can lid about 6 in. (15 cm.) from your face and look through at your friend—using the hole you punched like a gunsight. The light from the sun will then pass through the hole and you will see it reflected on your face as you look at your reflection on the shiny side of the lid which is facing toward you. Check that you still have your distant friend in line by looking through the hole. And then tilt the lid until the reflection of the sunspot on your cheek is guided back through the hole in the center of the lid. You are now flashing directly at your friend. If it was an aircraft or ship, your signal would be seen immediately.

Now supposing the angle between the sun and your friend is *more* than 90° (and not, as we have just seen, less). You will have to use a different way.

Method B

Balance the can lid upright across the palm of one hand—supporting it with the thumb—so that when you hold your hand in front of your face you can see your friend through the hole in the middle. Try not to let your fingertips get in the way. Now, to be able to signal your friend, you are going to have to hold the lid at a slanted angle. This is because the sun is well to one side, and may even be behind you. And you need to present the face of the "mirror" so that the sun will glance across it rather than bounce frontally from it, as in the last method. (Although this sounds rather complicated, you will soon catch the idea when you actually try it.)

Hold the lid, therefore, facing the sun, at first. And let the spot of light fall through the hole onto the palm of your hand. Now, swing the lid toward your friend so that its face is angling toward him. Look through your side of the hole. As long as you can see your friend, and as long as the spot of light still falls through the hole onto your palm, you are almost there. Keep an eye on your observer and tilt the can lid until the light spot disappears back through the hole. You are now flashing correctly—as your friend can confirm.

There is a third method of signaling for when you have only a broken piece of glass which can serve as a mirror. (Bottle glass, for instance, can sometimes send a dazzling signal.) Obviously here, you have no hole in the mirror for pinpoint aiming.

Tin-can-lid signaling

Method C

Hold the mirror up to the sun, and the other hand up in front of your face—arm outstretched—so that it blots out the view of your faraway friend. Tilt the mirror at different angles until you hit your other hand with a reflection of the sun from the mirror. Sight your friend through the slits between your fingers; keep the mirror flashing on that hand—and then lower it. You should now be sending a signal across to your helper.

Incidentally, it is easy to practice on your own. Paste aluminum foil to cover the bottom of a long, deep, and fairly narrow drawer. Place the drawer on one end of a table, chair, wall, hedge, or rock some distance away, and flash it with the three different methods outlined. When you hit the foil correctly, it will flash back.

FLASHLIGHT SAVING TRIALS

Go for long walks on dark evenings in your nearest countryside, and try these methods of obtaining the longest life from one set of batteries and one bulb in your flashlight.

A flashlight can look brighter when seen from a distance if it is reflected from snow or some form of mirror. Try it and see for yourself.

It is also more obvious if you keep it moving about.

A flashlight can be flashed to the rhythm of the Morse Code dots and dashes, or as the International Mountain Distress Signal. But, when you use either of these methods, know that the wear and tear on your bulb could burn it out. So press the ON/OFF button to "ON" and leave it there while signaling. Instead of switching "OFF," use your other hand as a shutter to place in front of the glass. Use the ON/OFF button when the battery is weak.

Beware of cold weather (or really hot temperatures) as battery life leaks away in extremes of climate. Boost fading batteries by keeping them warm next to your body, say, beneath your armpits for about half an hour.

Realize that battery-operated equipment needs nursing carefully and can easily go wrong. If you happen to have a powerful flashlight in an emergency, look on it as a real bonus and use it carefully.

SIMULATE A PILOT'S VIEW

Select a level site beneath (and it should not be directly beneath) the nearest high-level vantage point. This may be a steep-sided hill, a tall building or a cliff by the sea. You should next take turns in making ground-to-air signals on that level ground you chose. And you will be able to judge the effectiveness by looking down at your efforts from high above.

First, try all the ground-to-air signals as listed previously in this chapter. Make them on a *large* scale so they are readily seen from above. The materials you use are up to you, but they should be relevant to survival situations. For example, if your sport is canoeing, then you can concoct signals from the brightest pieces of gear which you would expect to have with you should you ever end up stranded on an island in mid-estuary: red sweater, orange life jacket, yellow parka, blue crash helmet, and so on. Try to make your signal contrast with its background of grass, sand, snow, rocks, or whatever it may be.

Second, try writing in snow or sand. Shuffle out the letters for "SOS" so that each letter is about 20 ft. (7 m.) tall. Then enlarge each letter by digging a trench for the "S," a trench for the "O" and a third trench for the second "S." Use a flat piece of stone as a shovel. Why? Because this is all you may well have in a real crisis. What is important, however, is that you pile the snow (or sand if you try this on the beach instead) dug from these trenches into the best position to cast sunlight or moonlight in long shadows along these letters. You can emphasize these shadows with soil, leaves, stones, and dirt in general so that each letter stands out when seen from above as if you are looking at it three dimensionally. When there is no snow or sand, then the letters for "S," "O," and "S" can be raised in relief by building them from low walls of rocks, foliage, and earth.

SOS shadow-writing signals

Finally, remember that any litter or rubbish or wreckage can add to your ground-to-air signals. Torn pieces of wreckage from a car, plane, or boat, for example, can catch sunlight and be seen from some distance in the sky, or by anyone who is walking over a higher skyline.

Do clear away your ground signals when you go. And try not to disturb the ground by trampling bushes, setting fire to grass, uprooting rocks, and generally vandalizing the terrain in practice. Of course, if you were really stuck in a survival situation, such measures would be valid. But not in practice, please.

SEASIDE SURVIVOR SPOTTING

Paddle a canoe or raft out across shallow water until you are some way from the river or pond or lake bank. (Only try this on safe, inland waters, or on placid stretches of coast and, of course, you should be a good swimmer.) Capsize your craft and swim back to the side. Now, swim back to your vessel and climb on top of it; wave a piece of clothing as a flag. (It works best if tied to an oar or paddle.)

Your friend, observing from the bank, will note two important things: that you were far too inconspicuous swimming to the side, for only your head shows above the water, and many potential rescuers in a real-life situation would miss sight of you, and that you are much more obvious to everyone in view, seated on your capsized vessel and waving a piece of clothing (even if it was your bikini).

Always remember if you capsize and/or are being swept out to sea with your vessel: STAY WITH THE BOAT AND SIGNAL FOR HELP. Trying to swim for the coastline means you lose contact with your boat which is still floating, you could easily be driven back and exhausted by an offshore current (or the wind), and you are not easily seen.

If you have several canoes, small boats, rafts, or other vessels, try this additional experiment. Let a number of people each take a craft and paddle it to different parts of a pond, tarn, or lake. Then have them all meet together and lash each vessel to one another in a circle with 20 ft. (7 m.) lengths of line. An observer will obviously find that everyone is much more visible when tied together. An aircraft pilot can spot lifeboats and rubber dinghies much more easily, following a shipwreck, when they are tied in a circle, than when they are separate and in the process of losing contact with each other, as well.

ROCKET AND FLARE PRACTICE

Only use fireworks in remote countryside that is well away from trees and, if possible, other people. You do not want to raise false alarms. And this is one form of signal, anyway, that needs little practice really because the instructions should be printed on the box containing these signals.

However, it does pay to have a working knowledge of pyrotechnic devices. These are of the following types:

White flares. Although they are not a distress signal, they can draw attention to you if you have nothing else but, say, a flag.

Red parachute flares. These can soar 1,000 ft. (300 m.) high and still send a glow through a cloud bank. Best used at night, they can be seen 50 miles away in good conditions. Beware of bits of hot metal dropping, though.

Star shells. They also work best at night. Watch for the Roman-candle effect as they hurl out stars that burn for several seconds way up in the sky.

Hand flares. (Some types can also throw out stars.) These can be seen for five miles or so, and are effective on cloudy, overcast days because they pinpoint your position.

Many rescues at sea and on mountains have only taken place because the survivor's very last flare was seen. So, do conserve your flares when in a tight spot. Do not blaze away regardless. Wait until you consider your chances of being seen are best. This might even be for a week or longer if you are in a really serious position. But, it will be worth it when that aircraft suddenly flies into view, and you can broadcast your predicament.

Take care if you do send up one or two rockets or flares in practice. Make sure the pyrotechnics are right way up for a start. Then aim them slightly downwind when firing—you do not want them to skim along horizontally and fail to reach a good height.

Although these fireworks go off without a bang or recoil, keep on your toes. If a flare, for example, is reluctant to go off, wait. Some flares take several seconds after you rip off the tab which ignites the blaze. If nothing happens after half a minute, throw water over the faulty firework and cover it with soil and stones.

Remember to take flares and rockets from their box or packet one at a time. Replace the lid or flap at once. Follow the instructions on each pyrotechnic carefully—like how to light flares at arm's length. And read these instructions with a flashlight, not a match or lighter, for safety.

8

TO MOVE
OR STAY PUT?—
AND SUNDRY OTHER
MATTERS

RETURNING to civilization is always better than staying holed up in your survival shelter. You can be a castaway for only so long without adequate warmth, water, food, or medical treatment—whatever your disastrous situation happens to be. There are cases of survivors today staying put too long.

However, do not rush into leaving the spot where, for the moment, you are reasonably safe and warm after meeting trouble outdoors. There are a great many dangers of going it alone.

That cross-country trek could turn into a nightmare if you become even more lost than ever and should conditions become worse. The state of the weather or the terrain or you yourself or your companions might deteriorate so badly that in the end you realize just how much safer you would have been had you, in fact, stayed put. There is always that chance, furthermore, that help might have passed the original place where you met with the accident . . . only by now you are no longer there. Certainly, setting out for help calls for preparation beforehand, a certain amount of physical fitness (no broken legs, say), and the fact that you do know where you are heading. Unless there is a road, town, or inhabited valley in the direction ahead of you, you would be better staying where you are and signaling for help. The one real exception to this is when you know exactly where you are, and also the route by which you can get help—especially when the distance is short. However, there are times—even when faced with what seems the longest march-out in the world—when it becomes apparent that you must make a move. An instance of this would be when you have spent several days or even weeks at the site of the accident, and your resources are exhausted. Everything has been used up—your bonfire fuel, matches, candles, water, and food. Then, in situations like these, when help just hasn't arrived, you must weigh all the pros and cons and decide to go look for it. It's a decision which can be very risky indeed to take, but once taken, give the measures toward achieving it everything you've got.

SHELTER AND WARMTH

Obtain whatever shelter you can as you go. It helps if you have already experienced living off the land personally. You are then so much better equipped mentally.

Somewhere near your home is an ideal survival site for the following important survival experiment (even though you may live in a big city).

Near every city and town you will indeed find rough country ideal for a bivouac. Make a reconnaissance there by bus, train, foot, or bike. Start in the public library by looking through guidebooks about the local countryside. If you live in a city, it is obvious you want the roughest country nearby (yet outside) your local community.

Instead of fields, riversides, and orchards, look for flats of grass among rock outcrops, fernbrakes, gorse bushes, chalk slopes, limestone scars, sandstone bluffs, stunted hawthorns, pine trees, glittering streams, white-sand strips, peaty wastes, and heathery horizons. Possibly you might find an aerial view of a township below like an airport seen from the sky.

Lonely backroad sites are better than those in city parks where you see too many people. Here no one will bother you. Your bivouac will be hidden in the backwoods terrain, and you need only ask permission if there is a farm nearby. If there is, you *must* ask.

Look for plenty of wood (avoid forests, though, because of the fire risk), a stream with fish in it and *above* any nearby houses (it should then be fresh), a spot to catch the sun in the early morning, high, dry, flat turf shielded by a wall, boulder, hedge, or trees (so your shelter can be made in its lee).

Avoid stagnant backwaters beneath water lilies or willows (which breed mosquitoes, mists, and chills), trees immediately overshadowing (they blot out the sun and attract lightning), long grass (it has bugs), clay, boggy or low-level ground (see stagnant backwaters), sandbanks (also see stagnant backwaters), horses, cows, and pigs which trample tents, canoes pulled out on riverbanks overnight and other people's possessions, busy roadsides, and rushing noisy water.

Having located a really good bivouac site and heard a good weather forecast for three days, begin. Wear old or outdoor adventure clothing (including your cagoule and a couple of sweaters). Take your boots, wrist watch, knife, and both survival kits. Remember, the survival kits are a reserve safety measure. Try at all costs to get through this survival experiment without having to open them.

You must begin the search for shelter materials growing naturally or lying on the ground. Use materials such as dead branches, long grasses, coarse ferns, heather, and, if at all possible, foliage already broken off. Because this is going to take some time, begin making your shelter in the morning rather than late in the afternoon—this will enable you to have a really thorough trial run.

To recap on shelter construction, there are certain specific requirements from the land around you. They come in many forms.

The natural umbrella of a few trees; the windbreak of ditchlike hollows; the wind and rain roof of plants with broad leaves like rhubarb and skunk cabbage; the building materials of bark slabs, conifer boughs, leafy deciduous branches, old logs lying exposed, small burrows, and piles of rocks. ALL can be used for shelter erection. Do pay extra attention to the bed, and use only the best ground-insulation material.

Crush a handful of green ferns, watch the juice drip, and make a mental note that a high-water-content vegetation makes poor bedding material. Instead go for dry grass, old holly, brittle bark, snappable wood and limbs, and crackling twigs. It must be dry and give invaluable dead air space between YOUR body and the cold ground.

> WARNING: In hot climates, you need to insulate yourself from scorching sand, grass, and weeds, as increased body heat is just as dangerous as body heat loss.

The next step is to collect loads of firewood (see chapter 3) and then concentrate on securing food for the night. Now comes the acid test as evening draws near, and you begin to feel apprehensive. It is so easy at this point to have second thoughts.

Survival experiments should be looked upon as the real thing. If you are tempted to give in without really trying, because some of them prove more difficult than you ever thought possible, you should examine yourself all the more closely. Not that this tendency means you would necessarily lack guts in a true-life drama, but it's just that you would be missing out on valuable knowledge learned from experience.

Of course, conditions may force your hand. And then one, or even both, of two things happen. You have to open your survival kit to get by for the night (yes, you use up the matches, food, etc., in it), or you can walk back to the bus stop, telephone, or bicycle and return home. Don't be put off. You will, at least, have now had firsthand experience of the psychological and physiological problems that accompany any survival situation, and this should give you food for thought and the highly likely human wish to try again.

ENERGY

SHELTER and WARMTH are vital survival attributes; they are also helped by anything which aids you to conserve, store, and boost your energy. Very closely linked with Shelter and Warmth (as we are about to discover during the construction of the shelter, gathering firewood, and lighting the bonfire), Energy is still the chief source which makes this section of survival possible.

Conserve your energy all the time by following these Ten Golden Rules as you go about surviving your two nights in the open.

Stay Dry. The weather forecast should see to this for you in advance. If it does rain hard, then you do have an excuse to cancel the experiment and try again at a later date when the weather is more favorable. At this stage, it IS risky for you to persevere in wet clothing which loses all its insulation.

Do Not Sweat. The climate could be rain free for days, but your body actually *rains* sweat onto the insides of your clothing and this continual shower of perspiration means you are wasting energy, as the extra heat to cause your sweat can only be ENERGY in use. Sweating also makes you thirsty, and you could be short of water.

Slow Down. In anything using muscle—shed building, wood splitting, log dragging, bed construction—try to set a slow speed.

Rest. Aim for a five-minute break at least every hour. The reason is that rest allows the muscles to get rid of waste products accumulated when you have been driving them cruelly. But avoid frequent arbitrary stops.

Drink Warmed Liquids. Swallow cold water and your energy processes have to heat it to body temperature— 98.6°. Drink warmed liquid and save calories.

Wear a Hat. Shepherds tending sheep on Christmas Eve are never bareheaded for they know the value of their headgear. The brain receives 20 per cent of the body's blood supply and 25 per cent of the oxygen intake. An exposed head, therefore, can leak away a large proportion of the body's heat—wasted energy.

Be Comfortable. If what you are doing does not feel right —or comfortable, even—you are not doing it correctly. Blue hands, red fingers, and a gray nose, for example, are NOT a green light for safety. They show you are losing body heat. Shield yourself from wind blowing away body warmth. Add clothing when the temperature becomes colder.

Do Not Panic. Good judgment is overruled by terror and imagination. Struck with fright, you panic and invaluable energy is wasted.

Wrist Watch Memo. Think of its jewels. Yet energy is by far your most precious possession in the wilds. And just as it can be conserved to sustain life for a long time, so can it be exhausted in a few hours—blown away by the wind or gulped up by the muscles if you are not very careful.

Eat. Nibble, chew, and swallow all the food you can find growing or living naturally wherever you happen to be—

as you go about propping up shelters, making fires, and searching for food and more food.

FINDING FOOD

Wherever and whenever you are in the countryside, test and try different natural foods. Some—the more repulsive sounding (like snails and frogs)—will not appeal until you are ravenous with hunger, but others (berries, nuts, and wild fruit) are the starters which will encourage you to think along the right lines.

There is a most important spin-off, too, when discovering and masticating the food you find that will give you ENERGY. For food gives WARMTH as well. The stuff you eat may be cold, but its proteins and carbohydrates will all help stoke up the furnace inside you by which you power limbs and body. Watercress of all things, for example, is rich in protein and—weedy and sodden, sorry-looking vegetation as it may seem on a windy day—can still be good fuel for your body-heater system.

A person basically healthy, and not too badly injured, should be able to live two hundred hours without sleep, go several days without water—unless he is in the desert—and several weeks without solid food. Yet, if you do not get *some* food, your body becomes "autocannibalistic" and begins eating itself away (first, carbohydrates, then your body fats, then proteins from your muscles and tendons). It may be several weeks before you die from lack of food, but your efficiency which is so vital in surviving through this period will be badly affected.

There are several experiments which will show you the way to live off the surrounding countryside when your own food supply is nil. But, first take heed of all those kinds of wildlife nutrition which are dangerous. And which can kill in some instances if you take so much as a bite.

It would fill a book to show all the dangerous and poisonous plants growing in different places. And even when you *think* you know your toxic vegetation, you can never be sure. Nevertheless, there is a way in which you can question and test for poisonous effects and you should use it for every herb, leaf, blade, sprig, frond, root or, berry when you have any doubts. Remember the sequence: SMELL, LOOK, TASTE, WAIT.

SMELL to check if there is any odor. If there is, then leave it alone.

LOOK to see if a milky juice can be squashed from the plant. If there is, forget about eating that plant.

TASTE for any immediate bitterness. If none, bite off a small piece and place it on the inside of the lower lip and leave it there for five minutes. Only when it still doesn't taste bitter, soapy, burning, or otherwise foul should you eat it.

WAIT after swallowing any morsel of strange plant food —for three hours. No stomach-ache? No sickness? Then the plant will be safe enough to eat in bulk.

No matter how hungry you are, always pause to heed this survival warning. It is a simple test which has proved safe in many wildernesses of the world, and it will let you distinguish between poisonous leaves, for instance, and nontoxic fronds, between berries like the bittersweet variety which can poison children and bilberries which stain your lips a bright purple but which do no other harm.

Leave all mushrooms alone, even when you *think* they will be safe. Only an expert can really tell. An instance of danger is in the belief that if you can peel it, you can eat it; the deadliest fungi, the death cap, is one of the easiest to peel.

Just as dangerous is to throw away caution because you see wildlife living off the land. Rabbits, goats, and blackbirds thrive on deadly nightshade, yet it is poisonous to man who has a completely different digestive system. And this is only one example. Test the vegetation foreign to you, and see if your own digestive system agrees with the five-minute tasting as outlined already.

Plants

Rose hips, nuts, roots, berries, seeds, pods, flowers, buds, leaves, stems, bulbs, shoots, sprigs, bark and so on . . . they can all be eaten. And although you may well pull a face now, such fare does prove more palatable when you have no other choice but to eat it. Eating plants is also going to be a more difficult choice for you at first than, say, chewing boiled snails or swallowing mouthfuls of dead insects and grubs. There is a snag, however; you need to eat a great many plants to gain any food value benefit. Simply gulping down a few handfuls of berries or pocketfuls of nuts is not enough.

Try these experiments and see for yourself.

Spear fruit

Wild strawberries, raspberries, and other fruit can be carried by the spearing method—take a long, thin piece of grass and push it through the centers of the wild fruit. Tie the grass ends and carry the hoops back to your shelter.

Remember, food like this which you don't need to wait to eat can help more unappetizing sustenance down—like the sugar coating on a pill.

Chew grass

While searching for food, use the reviving qualities of the juicy last half-inch stem at the bottom of the best grass. Just wind each head of grass around your index finger and pull. The most succulent ends come out clean, white, and firm (and taste like aniseed balls).

Mash grass

Pile grasses onto a piece of cloth on a flat rock and smack out the seeds with a stick, then wait until you have a fire and boil in water. Chew the stems while you work.

Crack eggs

No fresh egg is inedible. Wild birds' eggs have a stronger flavor because of the variety of food eaten by wild birds.

Dig pignuts

Crunchy chestnutlike bulbs can be rooted up from beneath small white flowers dotted around pastures.

Eat leaves

Sour dock leaves—a tiny version of the dock leaf—which grow in fields, and wood sorrel leaves—heart-shaped and bearing small white flowers—which grow in shady glades, are nutritious. Honeysuckle leaves, beech leaves, and other leaves are also worth eating so long as you try the poison test first.

Make salads

Crab apples, wild bullaces (like little damsons), beechnuts and hazelnuts (crack with a stone, not your teeth) can be mixed with watercress, wood sorrel leaves, fresh grass, young bracken shoots, the scraped-clean roots of young dandelions and primroses. (Scrub off the tiny hairs, however, which cover primrose stalks and which contain an irritant to sensitive human skin.)

Boil until tender

A whole variety of natural foods can be mixed into paste this way. Try the boomerang-shaped seeds off the ash tree which float twirling down to earth; pull off the ash keys and boil until quite tender. Also boil lichens scraped off rocks after soaking well first; the inner layer of tree bark (it can also be chewed raw); young coils of ferns after scrubbing off the hairs on the stems; seaweed *that clings to rocks* (the sign of safe-to-eat seaweed); nettles until they taste like spinach.

Make salt

Evaporate sea water with fire or sun.

Brew tea

Nothing tastes better than tea when you are cold and tired. The ritual of preparing the fire and having a cup of tea, by whatever means it is made, restores perspective. Teas can be made from almost any plant, and these can be fresh or dried. Infuse in boiling water for about ten minutes. Try with everything from pine needles to wild mint or even nettles. Honey—if you can find it—is a natural sweetener.

CATCHING FISH

Pike, like most fresh-water fish (try it with sharp-tasting weeds such as wood sorrel for seasoning), is edible. And this is only one example. Catch as many fish as you can using methods like the following.

Trout tickling

Many country schoolchildren have tickled trout during school playtime. You should try it too. Don't worry if the trout dart away during your approach. They will return to the stream banks after you have settled down to wait. After a time you can move your arms and the trout will probably ignore the movement. So long as you are by the deep parts of a stream or river, you can look under the overhangs of banks where the dirt has been washed out from underneath. You can also look in pools below shallow stream rapids, turning rocks over slowly.

One has to go about this with great care and calculated slowness. You must put your hand in very, very gently and move it beneath the water very, very slowly, for the slightest quick movement can frighten the fish. Feel gently until your hand touches a fish's tail. Stroke slowly along the body. Before you know it, your fingers will touch the underbelly which should be massaged softly and tenderly just behind the gills. In a minute or two, clasp it quietly with thumb and forefinger (still stroking) and the other fingers AND lift.

Here are two more tips. Place a handkerchief over your hand to get a better grip—this helps most when you have small hands. Second, be ready by the water at dawn and dusk which are good times for fishing (especially if you carry a flashlight which fish find hard to resist).

Before any form of netting or trapping, however, you must know the movements of the fish first. Sea fish move in with the tide, then swim along the shore. Lake fish swim for the banks, usually in the early morning and at dusk.

Where possible, therefore, pick your trap site at high tide and fix it at low tide. And remember—nets (like flags signaling SOS) work all the time. They are always worth placing. Traps, moreover, keep the fish fresh in captivity until needed.

> WARNING: Throw away fish that LOOK unhealthy, that stink, and that stay dented if you press a thumb into the skin. Other danger signs are when a fish has no scales, feels puffed up like a ball, and when it bristles with nasty spikes. Dead shellfish are also bad; they should grasp rocks or obviously move.

A fish trap

Trapping and netting fish

Thin supple branches can be shaped into a conelike basket with a narrow entrance to trap the fish. You may be able to think of other improvisations, like a string vest, say, which makes a good net. You can also make more fish traps from sticks and rocks as shown.

Fishing tests

Anything which can be used as a fishing line goes, and that includes not only your hooks but your bait and—if you can find one—your rod too. Let's take them in that order.

String, thin strips ripped from old shirts, bailer twine, electric wires and anything else of reasonably small diameter and fairly strong will suffice as a line. It helps if you can attach the hook end to fuse wire so that a fish's bite won't sever the lines when the hook catches its mouth.

Anything sharp and curved, or which can be bent into a curve, will do as a hook—pins, safety pins, bones, thorns, and stiff wire, for example. But do try to keep your hooks sharp.

For bait use what you can find around you such as worms, grubs, and grasshoppers, though some fish can be attracted

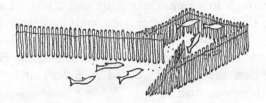

Another fish trap

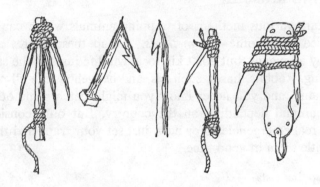

Alternative to fishhooks

with colored cloth, feathers, or even a small piece of bright metal.

Use a willow or any fairly long green branch to improvise your pole. Although it's easiest to tie the line to the end of the rod, a better idea is to thread any line which is long enough back along the rod through guides of wire loops which are bound at intervals along the rod. Just two or three of these supports for the line will do and will prove enough if a struggling fish snaps off the end of your pole. This way you don't lose the line completely as it is still attached at other points to the rod. Tie the end of the line—the opposite one from the hook end—around the handgrip of the pole.

Don't waste too much time and energy fishing with rod and line, however. It's a technique strictly for 1) when fish are plentiful enough to be caught readily and 2) you have done everything else at the site where you are a castaway and now you have nothing better to do. If the fish fail to bite, leave shorter fixed lines attached to a low branch or the riverbank (in which case they should be tied to floats) and do something else more worthwhile.

HUNTING ANIMALS

There are various methods of trapping animals which can be practiced near home—as *methods*. Set up these snares and traps by all means, but don't kill local wildlife just for the sake of killing. Rabbits, hares, squirrels, and hedgehogs are all possible game, and you never know you might catch some other larger animal depending on the country. But only consider this in real emergencies. For now, just set your traps and then dismantle them in good time.

Trapping tests

Methods of catching and killing elusive animals include snares (rabbits and badgers); sprung traps and nets; burning trees or small bushes to flush small animals out, sealing most warren holes with sticks and forcing the animals out of the remaining holes by means of smoke. Apart from not killing now, do not forget, also, that many methods are illegal, and many birds and animals are protected by law anyway.

However, you can experiment with these methods—stopping short of the kill. Set up the different traps as shown and practice the tactics you would need in a true emergency.

And there are always more direct methods too—like firing off a catapult which is powered by elastic from your underpants, and clubs made from heavy branches (you grip the slimmest end) and even bottles which come to hand. Then there is hurling rocks, not as unreasonable a method as it sounds if you have practiced throwing at old Coke cans after

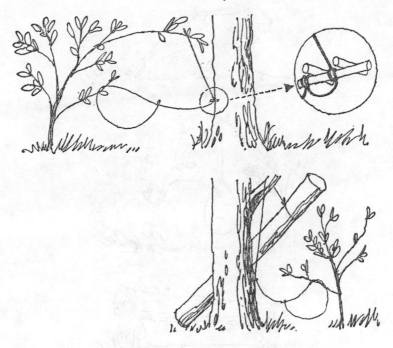

Two snares

waiting for sitting targets like hypnotized rabbits. *You* do the mesmerizing by sucking in air sharply through pursed lips. The squeak emitted will stop a rabbit in its tracks for a long moment or two, giving you ample time to take aim. And remember spears can be hurled javelin style if you have trained at letting fly with sharp-ended branches. Use cave men axes, too, made simply by binding a flat rock or slate into a strong cleft stick with a dead animal's skin cut into strips or whatever other binding material you may have handy.

Snares, traps, and deadfalls—many of which need a triggering device which the animal trips—can all be made in practice, and with no other materials than dead wood lying on the ground. They will not be effective, however, unless you know *where* to use them.

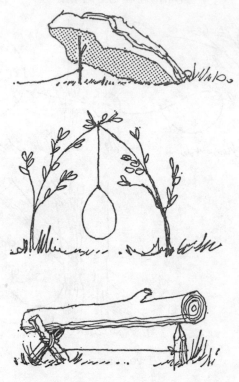

Three more snares or deadfalls

But when you do know, it is like the fishing lines left in the
water and anchored to a tree branch—they are always working for you while you carry on with other tasks, providing you
set them up correctly.

A snare is simply a loop of wire or cord (the latter is not so
good because it can break or be chewed through more easily)
placed in a position where the animal can run headlong into
it; and while the loop is big enough for the captive's head, it's
far too small for the body to pass through. The result is that as
the animal's forward rush is suddenly halted, the loop tightens
around its neck and strangles it to death.

The deadfall, however, depends on the animal tripping over

an outstretched cord or small poised branch or rock "trigger." As a result, this in turn dislodges a much heavier rock or tree limb which topples onto the victim and kills it.

As for placing your animal killers, set them in animal runways in the grass or shrubbery or snow, or at the openings of burrows, warrens, dens, and the like. Tracks and fresh diggings are the things to look for; as long as you can use them as the places for your snares and deadfalls—and not just anywhere chosen completely at random—all you then need is patience. Don't expect to catch anything the first day, nor even the second. You must be prepared to wait several days. But by spacing out different traps over as big an area of ground as possible, you certainly stand more chance of success. It helps, moreover, if you reinforce your traps by channeling animals directly toward them. To do this you just "fence" existing game runways with sticks, rocks, and vegetation so there are no escape exits, and once an animal is moving along that trail then it will be led inevitably to the snare, or whatever, ahead.

CASTAWAY COOKING

Aim for simplicity—you will have no choice in a bad situation. Your trial cooking could become too fancy, though, if you let your imagination run away.

It is wise to build a fire in a hole for cooking so that, once alight, it burns slowly and far longer—then you can keep it going and save matches. At first, stick to the kind of food you can cook at home so as to get the hang of preparing food in the open. Later, you can become more ambitious (and realistic).

So now you are cooking in your back garden or nearby field in preparation for spending your two nights out (when you will be cooking whatever you find out in the wilds and nothing else).

Green twigs make good forks for sticking into food which is being cooked over flames. And it's possible to boil water in a

Cooking aids

piece of paper folded so as to make a mug, or even by using birch bark layers and folding them paper-fashion.

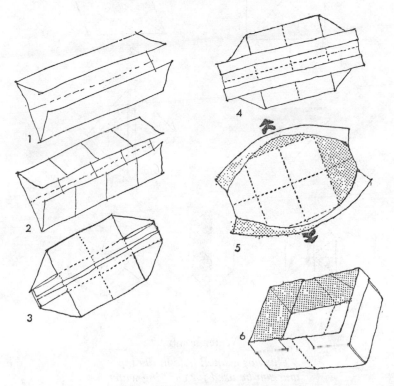

Paper pan for boiling water

At first cook what *you* like. It seems easier this way. Try some of these recipes too—just open canned food you like, heat and eat; prick an egg at the small end, set it upright in the coals (hole on top) and cook for twenty minutes; bake fish (you possibly bought it or caught it) in green leaves or aluminum foil beneath hot coals for fifteen minutes if small, or up to sixty minutes if large; cook steak laid out on coals that are glowing or between two flat rocks that are hot enough to splatter water off them with a hiss!—keep the fire going for

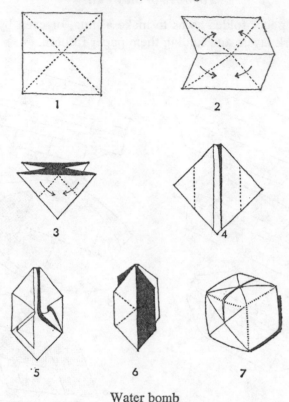

Water bomb

*This has a small hole in the top
and can be used for carrying water*

anything from thirty minutes to an hour; heat porridge that
has soaked overnight in salt and water; bury a big potato,
wrapped in mud or aluminum foil, in the edges of the fire for
thirty minutes.

Survival cooking

"Don't kill animals unnecessarily" was the advice given earlier. If, however, you do practice with snares and deadfalls,
and these "accidentally" yield dead meat, then make use of
this food as you would in a survival situation, and cook over a
small bonfire as before.

The safest rule is: cook *fresh* food you have just killed after letting the blood drain out and eat immediately. Cooking makes the food safer by killing off parasites and germs at once. Boiling is best. It preserves the juices; the cooking water is full of nutrients. And you can always add plants to fish or meat stew. But do boil sea food in salt water. Second best to boiling—some say as good, in fact—is to preheat a stone-lined pit with a fire, and then remove the embers. Wrap your meat in leaves or seaweed and place it in the pit. Now cover with more leaves and seal with a covering of soil. Unearth the food several hours later, and the meal will be ready.

Extra meat and fish cut into strips, can be dried in the sun or over a fire and stored. Another point, when you hang up a dead animal to let the blood drain, cover it up and keep it from being contaminated by flies. Wet leaves, damp moss (like sphagnum moss), or tree bark can all be used. And here are some examples of how to get dead carcasses ready for survival-type meals.

Hedgehogs

Roll the carcass in clay and bury beneath the embers of a fire for over three hours. This is easy to do if you first of all let the fire go low then remove the embers intact to another fireplace nearby. Dig into the ground beneath the ashes left behind, bury the hedgehog, then cover with the hot ashes and carry the embers of the fire back to this original fireplace too.

Shellfish

Mussels are risky in summer and can be poisonous. So only consider eating them from October through to April. They can be boiled or steamed. *Never* touch shellfish that are already dead or among numbers of dead ones lying around. You should put clams, mussels, and crabs in a clean pool first, and they will clean themselves.

Frogs

Strip away the skin which contains glands toxic to humans before cooking.

Crows, wood pigeons, and other birds

You can eat them all, and the fats in their skin are highly nutritious. So: 1) break their necks by wringing them in both fists; 2) pluck them warm; 3) let them hang to allow the blood to run into the head; 4) cut out the bowels; 5) chop off the head; 6) cook spit-fashion over flames on a green stick and eat by picking at them so as to get those valuable fats inside yourself.

Trout and other fish

Break the fish's neck by jerking its top teeth upward with your thumb. Cut along the underside, and run a finger inside the slit to disembowel it. Wrap in wet leaves or seaweed and bury in the ashes (as described above) after first cutting the head and tail away.

Snakes

These are good when cooked. First, cut off the head, remove the entrails, and take the skin off.

Rabbits

A karate-type blow across the back of the neck just behind the ears will kill. Then slit the underside and disembowel with your fingers. Hang—like a dead bird—to let the blood drain. Then unroll the skin glove-fashion (removing the head too). The meat should be knifed into small squares which can be cooked over the fire on green twig stickers.

WATER

You *must* find water in any drought-hit climate. This does not have to be desert either. It may be grasslands burned dry in the sun, or a frozen mountain, but you do need water. Humans can go without water for a few days only, whether the weather is hot or cold, yet go without food for weeks and still struggle through.

SOME WAYS OF FINDING WATER

Water diviners use various techniques to locate water underground—from a forked twig to a pendulum (a coin swinging on a length of thread). You can find water too, using far more basic methods. Try these. . . .

Save the water in your body (the human body is around 80 per cent liquids) on a very hot day. First, drink as much water as you can. Then go outside on a sunny day and read a book.

Button up your clothing. This makes you uncomfortable, but it stops you sweating so much, and it prevents you pouring out vital body moisture. Lie in the shade of a wall. Despite the heat—and although you imagined you would grow tremendously thirsty because your clothing is fastened (no short shirt sleeves, for instance)—you will not need a drink all day.

This, of course, is because you are saving the water inside you, *which is where it counts.* Just taking sips from a bottle of water during the day is nowhere as effective as *filling yourself up with water first,* then sitting still. But supposing you must walk across dry and arid wastes with the sun scorching down? The answer is, if it's going to be any real distance, wait. And when dusk falls you can begin your trek then in the cool of the evening.

Now let's turn to other experiments in collecting fresh water from as many different sources as possible. We should try to tap them all.

Test which receptacles collect rainwater best—pieces of cloth lining a hole dug in the ground, small plastic bags hung open on tree branches and supported by twig ends, Wellington boots and hats left out in the rain, a drainpipe made from strips of cloth ripped off old shirts and knotted together so that hanging from a tree branch or, preferably, a leaning tree trunk, it rains water downward into any available container.

Leave shiny objects out at night such as silver foil, the glossy side of a tent groundsheet, car hubcaps, large slippery leaves, and smooth stones. Then get up early and take a sponge with you to soak up the moisture which has collected.

Place snowballs on anything dark-colored that will hold water—such as in a plastic bag resting on a dark coat. Then let the sun melt them.

Try boiling ice. This is not as easy as it sounds. While producing more water than snow, ice nevertheless will vanish into nothing if you simply place it in a container and heat over a fire. The answer is to have a little water in the bottom of the container to start off with, then add chunks of ice (or pieces of hard-packed snow taken from beneath the surface crust).

You must never touch sea water. It will dehydrate your body quickly and make you even more thirsty than before no matter how cooling and refreshing it may seem at first. *Never ever* drink from the sea.

There are only two possible uses for sea water. The first is to wipe your face occasionally as a help in cooling you down. The second is that the high-tide level on a beach will give you a clue as to the possible whereabouts of fresh water. Then you can try this next experiment.

Wait until low tide, then dig in several places in the sand with a shell or lump of driftwood both above and below the high-tide-level mark. Fresh water can often be discovered just beneath the sand as it is lighter than salt water and tends to float on top. Make a note of the position of your find (above *or* below the high-tide level, determining the whereabouts of, which is the purpose of this experiment). And don't dig too deeply, or you will hit the salt water. The fresh water—actually, it will taste brackish—should be sucked up a straw, hollow grass, or any kind of tubing you have available if possible.

Make a solar still in your back yard or in any convenient waste piece of land. It will give some results, even though it is really meant for use in hot desert country where there is no water whatsoever and so you must manufacture your own supply. Or, it can be used to purify existing water such as urine, sea water, or almost any other kind of water which is

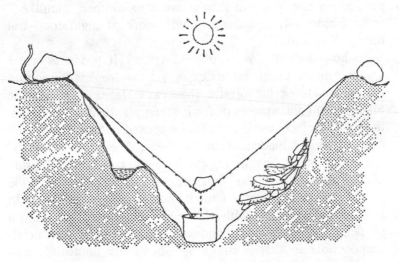

Solar still

undrinkable and dangerous (because it is so tempting to sip it when you are going crazy with thirst).

As shown in the diagram, you must first dig a hole shaped like a basin in the ground. It can be about 3 ft. (1 m.) in diameter (or rather more if you wish) and, say, 2 ft. (0.5 m.) deep. And do locate this still in a low-lying area in relation to the rest of the surrounding terrain. You don't want any shade around either, because the idea is that you cover this hole with a plastic sheet and the sun's rays then pass through this to be soaked up by the soil beneath. The result is that the earth's moisture under the plastic evaporates. The water vapor this produces condenses on the underside of the cooler plastic and drips into a container below. And of course even more water is then drawn to the topsoil beneath the plastic to replace the moisture which has evaporated already. Because of this capillary action a solar still can produce anything from around one to three pints of drinkable water in the driest desert. What's more, if a still begins to slow down in its production rate, you can then move it to another "unmilked" area. Incidentally, a solar still will work at night too—but only half as well.

So how does it purify polluted water? It produces water vapor from the undrinkable liquid and the droplets formed on the underside of the plastic sheet are *clean*. By the same token, if you place pieces of fresh green plants in the hole too, the moisture from these can also be sucked out under hot sun, evaporated and condensed on the plastic sheet.

First, however, having dug the hole, cut a trench in the side of this basin to hold the "contaminated" water such as urine or old car-radiator water (but it must not have antifreeze in it). Carefully line this with plastic sheeting as you would in a proper survival situation and raise the edge of the bowl-shaped hole so that it sticks up above the immediate surrounds (reason: to raise the plastic cover at the edges so that, if it rains, dirt won't be swept onto the sheet and foul the clean rainwater trapped there as a secondary drinking source).

Fill the trench you made with polluted water—such as dirty washing-up water. Also, add those newly chopped bits of greenery mentioned before, and lay them in the basin on the other side. Then position a bowl, tin can, or some other receptacle on the floor of your hole to catch the drips of condensation from the plastic sheet above. There is one thing more to do here, however, before you place the plastic sheet across the hole: arrange a length of rubber or plastic tubing leading from the container up to, and over, the edge of the hole in the ground. This will let you drink from the container without having to take up the plastic sheet. In fact, you should try leaving the plastic in place all the time since every occasion you do have to lift it, the condensation process has to start from scratch again.

Now stretch the plastic across the top of the hole. Anchor it in place with heavy rocks and seal any gaps with soil. Place a stone in the center so that the sheeting is pulled tight, yet at the same time it should not sag so sharply that it touches the sides of the holes nor brushes against the container. Leave it for the sun to activate.

The water you obtain from a solar still is fit to drink, but any water that already exists in natural surroundings, and which hasn't been produced by you, should be treated with suspicion. You need to purify it. The best way to do this is by boiling. Try it now with rainwater but first filter the water through a piece of cloth or slice of bread (assuming you have some). After ten minutes, take the rainwater off the boil and drink it as it cools. That's right, it tastes insipid. However, if you try this test again but throw a few pieces of charcoal from the fire into the water at the beginning, you will notice a much sweeter taste. (You will need to filter the water again after boiling in this case.)

TOOLS—AND DOING WITHOUT THEM

Making your way to safety needs all the various help you can muster en route. Therefore, under the heading, TOOLS, comes all the improvisations and methods of using outdoor equipment you would have been most careful to bring along had you known this crisis was going to fall: a compass, for example, or a pair of dark glasses to combat snow glare.

If, on the other hand, you did not have all the gear—you were skiing, for instance, and lost everything in an avalanche —here is how to make do with whatever you can find on your long trek back to civilization.

Crossing rivers has contributed to as much sudden death as any falls from rock faces. World-wide statistics show it. While water canoeists know the hideous power in floodwater—that surge which will submerge a grown man in water only knee-deep by hurling him off his feet.

Many mountains are moated by water after heavy rain. Then the desperate crossing maneuvers begin. Commando exercises are not in it. There are safety rules, but they will not guarantee your life. Much the best way, if at all possible, is to detour, possibly miles, around mountain rapids. If not possible, here is how to take the plunge.

The easiest place to ford a mountain stream has the following criteria: it is shallow; the banks are easily climbable; there are no dangerous rocks, waterfalls, rapids, sluices, whirlpools, or reefs downstream so that if you do get swept off your feet, you will be hurled upon or into them; the current should NOT be at its strongest point. Such river and stream crossings will usually be found best where the watercourse divides into separate waterways with shingle or boulder islands in between.

Have a good look at the types of current. V-shaped ripples with the narrow end upstream mean rocks just beneath the surface of the water. W-styled formations of ripples, however, stand for two submerged rocks with a clear channel between them. Slowly circling water currents—perhaps with foam on top—are a sign of slack water. Test how deep these are with a long stick or pole (which can also act as a third leg as long as you jab it hard on the upstream side of the riverbed as you put your weight on it while bracing against the force of the current). Remember, it's better to go from slack water to a quicker current than to head from a swift current toward still water on the far side. Another point is that water moving slowly means it is deeper, and whether or not you decide to cross it depends on how confident you feel in water. Don't be too confident, though; use that long branch as a third leg for probing.

Keep boots and clothing on. A rucksack will help your balance, and if packed properly can be a buoyancy aid too if you overbalance. Just make sure you can whip it off your shoulders quickly if needed.

Pocket your wrist watch. Then take short and shuffling steps facing the far bank. Hang on to boulders where available. (Some will be submerged, but they are still useful holds.) *Never* face downstream—the weight of the current behind your knees can make your legs buckle. Keep facing across to the opposite bank, and avoid crossing your legs. But if the current becomes too powerful, move down and across to the riverbank farther downstream. Go, to some extent, with the current.

Weak, exhausted, or inexperienced companions should get between two strong people, arms linked. The strongest person is upstream, the rest of the chain arrayed below and parallel with the current—all making for the far bank and facing that way. Best results here are when using a pole or long branch as a rail, everyone grasping it, arms still linked.

Only use a rope as a last resort. If hung out as a hand line, make sure it is draped clear of the water. Never tie it around someone's waist then pull it in from upstream if he slips. Pay it out, swinging the swimmer to the side.

DON'T PANIC—THINK CLEARLY

The chances of being found quickly after an accident are excellent today, especially if you have told someone where you were going. Within a few minutes of the telephone reporting that you have not returned, a search party of trained men will be organized. Should the call be made at dusk, however, the searchers could well wait for two or three hours in some terrains because many people reported lost have merely been delayed and come out of the wilds by themselves.

Calm down panic as soon as you realize you are lost. You will feel you want to run, but check yourself. Now is the time to do things slowly and calmly. Your energy—remember—is the most valuable thing you have. Save it.

Although it seems incredible, here are some examples of what people lost in woods, hills, and on remote tracts of open country have done when they found themselves completely lost and far from home: peeled off their clothes and sprinted for what they imagined was the way back (also imagining they would travel lighter too and so becoming victims of cold and rain); abandoned rucksacks and wandered in circles until found collapsed in deep snow; became so bewildered they failed even to follow rescuers who had eventually discovered them and were leading them to safety (they had to be led by ropes); climbed UPWARD along the banks of mountain streams in the belief they were following the water downhill; even hid from rescuers in case those rescuers were mad at them.

As an experiment, walk with a friend in an area you both know well. Head for the thickest wooded area and then separate. Not only should you both head in different directions well away from the main path, but one of you should wait for five minutes to let the other person get well and truly out of sight. You should have made an arrangement to meet at some rendezvous point which is familiar to you both, but meanwhile you must try to meet up with each other before this distant point is reached. This, after all, puts you in the position of someone who is really lost and who has strayed away from his companions by accident. Now you are trying to re-establish contact just as if you were adrift in the jungle or on mountains. The basic survival action in such an instance is always the same:

1. STOP.
2. BUILD A PILE OF ROCKS.
3. TRY TO THINK BACK TO THE POINT WHERE YOU WENT WRONG.
4. SCRATCH A MAP ON THE GROUND WITH A STONE OR TWIG.
5. WALK BACK ALONG THE WAY YOU THINK YOU CAME—BLAZING THE WAY AS YOU GO.

By blazing the trail, I mean cutting nicks at eye level into tree trunks (don't do this in practice, please, for ecology reasons), sticking twigs into the ground, laying down stones at strategic points, and generally marking out your retraced footsteps as much as possible. Now, supposing you still fail to meet up with your partner, or don't hit the main path, then return along your present route to that pile of rocks which you built when you first realized you were lost. Were this a true-life situation, you should then—presuming it's getting toward the end of the day—prepare a bivouac for the night and bed down until the next day. You will then have plenty of time from dawn onward to scan the surrounding countryside from a hill, or knoll, or rock outcrop and so either spy smoke from your companion's fire or see other signs of life. Failing this, you would then at least have a better idea of the best way to walk out of your predicament solo—say, by descending to a valley-bottom stream or river and following that down to civilization. As it is, however, you are only in a park or local woods, so you simply rendezvous at that agreed point with your friend as a last resort should you fail to find each other before then.

Never, by the way, follow a stream downhill closely. It will crash down through ravines en route. But keep near enough to its course to be able to trace where it meets the main watercourse in the valley, and follow that. This will lead to people and houses.

To discover the direction where a lake spills through its outlet—and it is not obvious—wait until a calm spell then float seeds or twiglets on the water. Check which way they drift. While performing this experiment, you can also try out various methods of direction finding. Check each one with an accurate compass.

Float a needle to find the way

Remember the needle you magnetized? (See chapter 3.) Fill the washbasin in your bathroom with water and lay a piece of Kleenex on the top of the water so that it floats. Place the needle on top of this, then press on the tissue with a finger so that it sinks. The needle will remain floating, however, and it will then swing around to settle in a position pointing north-south. (Which end does point north? . . . Well, if you've already forgotten, see chapter 3, or check with a proper compass held some distance away.) The one snag, of course, is that in a proper crisis you probably won't have any paper tissues with you, so use a leaf instead.

Using your wrist watch as a compass

As long as the sun is throwing shadows, and your wrist watch is set to Greenwich Mean Time, you can find north from the pointers.

Point the hour hand to the sun. Divide the angle between the hour hand and "12." This segment of your dial now—bisected as you just have done—points south (in the Northern Hemisphere). It is least accurate when the sun is overhead.

Steer by the sun

You can always tell north and south by the sun. Simply push a short branch into the ground *in the morning,* and from the top of the shadow it casts, draw a circle. To get a true ring, you really need some form of line—cord, string, shoelaces tied together, belt, or anything else with which it can be tied on to a sharp object, stone, or bit of wood so as to transcribe the circle on the ground. Now mark with a cross scratched with a rock the exact tip of the branch's shadow as it is at this moment. From now until noon, the shadow will begin shortening, but after twelve o'clock it will begin to lengthen again. Mark with a stone the place where once more it touches the circle you marked out. Look for the halfway point along the edge of the arc between the two points you have noted and scratch out a line from here to the branch sticking up in the center of the circle. As you look along this line out over the branch you are now gazing exactly south (the opposite being true for the Southern Hemisphere).

How to find north by watching stars

Pick out any bright star alone in an open part of the night sky and aim along a stick, pole, or branch as if sighting along a rifle in a cowboy film. Prop your elbows on a wall or rock or

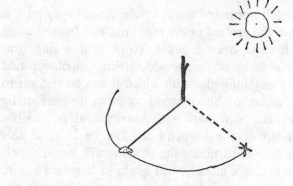

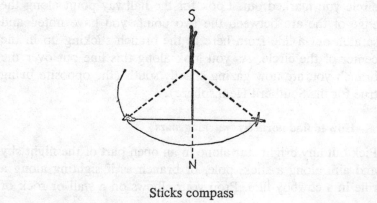

Sticks compass

tree to keep them absolutely steady. After a minute you will see the star move—an effect caused by the earth rotating. Check the following movements with a compass.

STAR ASCENDS = you are facing EAST

STAR DESCENDS = you are facing WEST

STAR SHIFTS RIGHT = you are facing SOUTH

STAR SHIFTS LEFT = you are facing NORTH

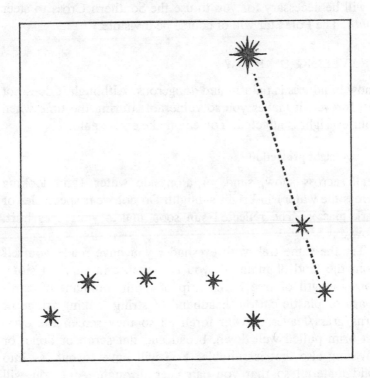

Great Bear and North Star

This little experiment is remarkably accurate once you have practiced and know the very slight movement to expect. You really do need to watch out for it along your "gun barrel."

Find the North Star, otherwise known as Polaris, in the Northern Hemisphere night sky and that's the north as bright as if electrically lit. The diagram shows how to look for the group of stars which point toward it—the Big Dipper and Great Bear constellation. Gaze into any clear dark night and you will always see them, providing you are in the Northern Hemisphere; and from these stars you can check the whereabouts of Polaris instantly. Practice first with a compass held in one hand to check. If you live in the Southern Hemisphere, it will be necessary for you to use the Southern Cross to steer *south*. The Pole Star will of course be invisible.

TRAVELING ON SNOW

Snow blindness is painful and dangerous. Although it does not last forever, it makes you so vulnerable during the time when your eyesight is affected. You can make errors galore.

Eyesight protection

Walk across snow, sand, or alongside water (and looking across the water) in bright sunlight. Do not wear spectacles or dark glasses. The reflected sun soon makes your eyes hurt. Now . . .

Try the same trek with eyeshades you have made yourself from the kind of materials you can expect in survival situations—length of tree bark, strip of cloth, remnant of cardboard or plastic carton, headband of string locking fringe of ferns/grass/leaves to your forehead so they screen the eyes, hat brim pulled well down, broad and flat scrap of bone, or anything else that is suitable. You will have to cut Xs into solid material so that you can peer through. And you will need to tie your shades in place with string or a few strands of elastic "borrowed" from your underpants.

Walk the same distance again, but this time with no eye-shades. Simply rub soil, dirt, or soot (from a fire or motor's exhaust pipe) right around your eyes (on the cheeks too). You will find that you have still cut down much of the glare bouncing up from the snow, sand, or water.

Float on powder snow

The softest snow is a menace to the traveler. He will sink up to the thighs or waist and expend so much energy that half a mile's slogging brings him to his knees. But supposing this was YOU on your way to fetch help for an injured friend?

Try these methods the next time you have a fall of snow. And do them before the snow has a chance to freeze really hard, or just wait until hard-frozen snow begins to thaw.

Search nearby woods for broad pine branches. Select two large, strong ones. Tie them to the soles of your boots with string, and walk across the softest snowdrifts you can find. They are clumsy, but they will support you.

Use *any* flat objects you find at home and try to tread snow with them. Tin trays, cushions, cake-tin lids, scraps of wood have all been used.

Tie green saplings—say, from willow trees—into two separate hoops (one for each foot) with string as shown. Given a cold enough winter you would need to thaw these, their sap frozen hard, over a fire. Drill holes through the hoops and construct a mesh of leather bootlaces by threading them through in a crisscross pattern. Again, the diagram shows the idea. The crosspieces supporting your foot should be as rugged as possible.

There are two important points. Don't make your snow-shoes too big. The smaller and lighter, as long as they do support you over soft snow, the better. Also, attach the snow-shoes to your feet with a broad strap fabricated from anything handy. You could just use string, of course, but a band of something like canvas, plastic, or leather is best because it is easier for such a fastening to comply with a key principle of snowshoe walking—the bands over your insteps must let the front of the snowshoes flip upward as you lift each foot so that the tail of the snowshoe drops back and trails in the snow. Experiment and you will see how important this is; it saves a great deal of effort. Snowshoes which are clamped rigidly to the soles of your shoes are literally a drag and need much more effort to walk over soft snow. All you have to do is to stride a bit farther, higher, and wider than usual. Your feet don't have to be too far apart, though, as the inner edges of the frames glide over each other as you step along.

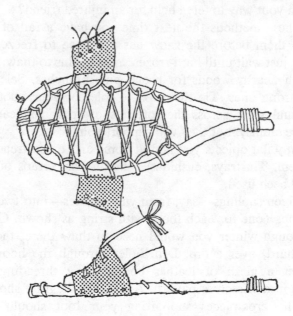

Improvised snowshoes

SPECIAL NOTE ON THE DANGERS OF HYPOTHERMIA

Exposure, or hypothermia, means the victim is dying from being too cold—not on the surface of the body—but deep inside him, in the body's inner core. If the temperature of this is lowered, BEWARE! And it has a final stress in this book, because its effect is so sneaky and yet is present in very many surroundings which have SURVIVAL connotations.

It is an all too frequent cause of death in the Great Outdoors, and it gains priority here over other kinds of accidents because it is such a cunning threat. It is not always easy to be sure that somebody IS suffering from mild exposure which can develop so seriously and so quickly, whereas with someone who has fallen and cut their head open the cause and effect are obvious.

THREE FALLACIES

"EXPOSURE" is the usual description, but its condition has no definite medical meaning. "HYPOTHERMIA" is the correct term.

VERY LOW TEMPERATURES alone do NOT cause hypothermia. People have died from hypothermia on a cold day in midsummer, babies in carriages included.

ALTITUDE does not matter either. You can die from the effects of hypothermia in a field.

It is a *combination* of causes that make you vulnerable to this dreaded killer in wild country. Singly, they are nowhere nearly as deadly as when they gang up on the unsuspecting.

Cold + Wind + Wetness + Fatigue = Hypothermia

Remember, the cold need not be extreme, the dampness need be caused by no more than condensed sweat inside your clothing (it need not be actually raining), the wind does not have to be gale force, nor do you have to be on your hands and knees with exhaustion. It is the COMBINATION of all of these factors, however, that accentuates each one.

Hypothermia has certain giveaway signs when you know

what to look for. It also helps to know the person who is in its grip, because he will always act out of character. If a person is a stranger, then a certain lackadaisical attitude may be just his own normal behavior. And *you* do not know him any differently. But if you are with a friend who is normally energetic and enthusiastic, but who begins to slur his speech, stagger, swear, shiver, complain about walking and wants to sit down . . . then these could be the signs and symptoms of hypothermia gaining a hold. In fact, a hypothermia victim tends to act drunkenly or high, and these signs become more obvious if the condition is not treated quickly.

Go over what the person you suspect is suffering from hypothermia is wearing and what he has eaten. For example, anyone who has eaten a hot breakfast and who has chewed energy-giving food like chocolate, raisins, dates and nuts through the day is unlikely to be affected by exposure. If he has kept drinking plenty too—even cold water—then the chances of his succumbing to hypothermia are less. Layers of wool clothing topped with wind- and rain-proof clothing in bad weather should save him from feeling any effects of the killer condition, too. However, if someone is wearing jeans and a shirt only on a bitterly cold day on the hills, then any sudden change of normal behavior could well be the advance signs of hypothermia striking home against the most foolish and vulnerable.

It is too late now, however. The damage is done. What can you do when somebody is showing these signs and symptoms?

Weigh up the situation. Is help or safety near? If only fifteen minutes away, say, everyone can help the affected person reach safety through encouragement, reassurance, and support. However, if there are several miles to go—stop. Get out of the wind and into shelter. Put up a tent if you have one, or find refuge behind rocks, trees, or a wall. If nothing else, use rocks piled high, a snowdrift, a wall built from large snowballs, or rucksacks placed on top of one another.

The victim must be kept warm. *At all costs YOU should try to prevent the further loss of body heat from the victim.* Pile clothing beneath him to stop the deadly cold striking upward from the ground. And then drape him with clothing too—any spare garments that are available as well as clothing.

If you have a sleeping bag with you, use it. The bag should be preheated by another member of the group who has stripped down to his underclothes so as to transfer a good proportion of warmth from his own body to the bag. And when the sleeping bag is sufficiently large, then that person can lie inside it with the hypothermia victim.

When there is no sleeping bag and no fire, a group of people should huddle around the victim so that their combined body warmth protects his failing body heat. And if there are only YOU and the hypothermia sufferer, embrace him until help arrives—supposing that there is no way you can go for help and leave the victim well wrapped up in sleeping bag or clothing—is the only answer.

Warm fluids like tea, broth, warm sweetened fruit juice, or any other soothing beverage should be handed around to others besides the patient. Candy, sweets, or anything else sugary are also good for the victim if he is able to eat.

There are several very important NEVERS, however, which you must know.

NEVER try to rub heat back into a hypothermia sufferer.

NEVER use hot water bottles or any form of hot water heating.

NEVER give alcohol to the victim.

NEVER use fire as a source of heat.

All such methods are dangerous. They release a sudden rush of freezing blood from the surface blood vessels which heads straight for the inner core of body warmth (already cooling under the hypothermia attack) and chills it even further—often fatally.

9

HOW TO HELP
SOMEONE ELSE

Survival is a warm body—yours. That is basically what the word "survival" means. When someone else's life is in danger, here is what you can do to help. You must make sure first, however, that your own body is warm enough to be able to afford the energy to help him—otherwise two people may well die instead of only one.

There is nothing that shows this important survival principle more than lifesaving in water, when you have never had lifesaving lessons and either cannot swim at all or at best can just manage to thrash out a few strokes.

LIFESAVING

Successful lifesaving depends on your being able to swim powerfully. If you cannot swim strongly, or—again, to labor a point which can never be stressed too much—even if you can, but have NOT had lifesaving instruction, do NOT go in the water.

Time and time again people drown when they go to the assistance of others. They forget that it takes knack, skill, and strength to tow or drag a drowning certainty to safety. Moreover, that person is struggling and resisting with the vigor of a maniac. A drowning man will clutch at a straw and, to him, you are that straw.

The experiments in this section all depend on YOUR being out of the water. You can still do what you can to help when you are on dry land and a person some distance away is drowning.

The business of getting to grips with a drowning victim in water, however, has no place here. You should learn this in the lifesaving courses run by your local lifesaving society. Aim to become a qualified lifesaver. It is an invaluable skill.

Lifesaving from bank, bridge, or beach

Remember, DO NOT JUMP IN. You would be amazed how instinctive this desire to help is in many people who see a person about to go under deep water for the last time. You are not a lifesaver, however, and instead should help in the ways the following experiments show.

Assess drowning spots

Look at rivers, ponds, canals, and lakes, or whatever the water near you at any time happens to be, from a new angle. Imagine you can see someone drowning whenever you are near deep water. Try to evaluate how you would be able to reach them *without* going into the water. Is there anything that floats nearby which you could throw? Is it shallow enough to be able to wade out part way to help? Is there any form of boat? Or might you be able to reach out with some object which they could grab?

Is there any other help available? How much current would you have to contend with? And wind—is it likely to interfere with your rescue attempt? Are YOU, yourself, fit enough to plow out in the shallow water you see and lug back a frantic friend (and supposing the shallows suddenly fell away over a deep shelf)?

Make a habit of doing this survey. You may be on a daily bus route which borders a river, or walking along a reservoir bank on the way to school, but wondering what you would do does help prepare you that little bit more. For then IF you did see someone drowning, you would carry out what you can practice in further lifesaving experiments. And in this order, for it has been found that the best way to save a drowning person from the land is first to try to reach them with something solid and, failing this, then to try the other choices listed below.

Reach out tests

Lie down flat on the side of a swimming pool, hold on to some secure anchor with one hand and reach for the victim. Impossible? Then extend your reach with anything handy . . . a stick, brush handle, piece of clothing, or a towel.

Discover, too, how when there are more than two of you involved, it is possible to make a human chain to reach the victim.

Throwing trials

The "victim" should go into the middle of the pool. Throw any buoyant object to which he can hang on—inflated life preserver, polystyrene float, or any other buoyant object within reach. If a line can be tied to the object first, you will be able to pull the victim to safety. Rather than throwing directly to the person in trouble, chuck just to one side. And practice throwing a rope cowboy style at a distant target in any spare moment.

> WARNING: Make a point of telling your "victim" that you are going to look for something to throw. A person who is really drowning will think you are leaving him if he sees you turn your back. Make it a habit to shout encouragement.

Wading experiment

Dash through the shallow end of a swimming pool to the "victim" who is on the far side. Make sure you grab him, rather than let the other person take hold of you. And watch your balance all the time.

Rowing tryout

Do this whenever you are by water where there are boats. Your "victim" should hail you from some distance out. Row or paddle out to him, and let him grab the boat or canoe so that you can tow him back to dry land. Approach him bow first (or, possibly, stern first) so he grasps an end and not the sides of the vessel which could capsize you. Warn him about climbing in—again, he can tip the craft over. Just paddle him ashore while he is still in the water.

Swimming probe

Swim to your "victim," holding some sort of support. This could be an inflated life preserver, a lifejacket, a polystyrene float, or article of clothing or a towel. Hold it in front of you. Avoid getting into physical contact, but offer the support ahead of you. Then you can swim back and pull him.

When someone else falls through ice

Fight down the urge to go out to the ice and pull someone clear who has just fallen through. Instead, tell the victim that you are going to help him if only he can hang on. Look for anything with which you can reach out to him: tree branch, pole, park bench, piece of fencing, ladder, roll of wire netting, length of drainpipe, bike . . . anything which he can grab while you—still on solid ground—pull the other end. If there is nothing rigid available, then look for a "rope" of some sort: hose pipe, scarves tied together, long chain, coil of wire (even barbed wire), wire netting possibly ripped from fence posts, electrified wire fencing—the type used to give cattle and sheep a mild shock if they stray too near the edge of their grazing (what is a small electric shock as you wrench the wire free compared with saving a life?) . . . any of these can be tied at one end to a rock, shoe, or some other weight and slid out across the ice to the casualty who is struggling in the water. When joining different "ropes," however, do remember to tie proper square knots, otherwise your rope will break when the tug-of-war to get the person out of the water begins.

There is one more method which is very much a last resort. When there are several onlookers, they can form a human chain by lying on the ice. One person squirms ahead, prone first of all, and someone holds his ankles. Then, when the first person has wriggled out onto the ice, the next person follows, still holding the first person's legs; his ankles in turn are held by a third person. And so the human chain advances across to the victim. As soon as the first person is near enough he hands a belt or some piece of clothing tied into a loop to the victim. Once this has been grabbed, the human lifeline backs toward the edge of the water, everyone pulling back on the person in front of them. Of course, it is important to have people still on firm ground so they are able to pull the chain of helpers back all the more quickly, and anchor them.

Two final factors always help. First, tell anyone who is in this predicament to grasp the ice which has not yet collapsed until you can reach him, and to kick hard with the feet as if doing the breast stroke. Second, a ladder is the best rescue aid of all if you can find one long enough to reach.

SURVIVAL FIRST AID

First aid to companions who have met with an accident outdoors should be kept to the very minimum until help arrives.

However, never underestimate an injury to the extent of leaving it completely unattended until a rescue team does arrive.

The danger is in being too zealous, and trying to help too much. Hospitals invariably wish many first-aiders would dress down their efforts which are well-meaning, but often wrongly applied and harmful.

Do the *least* you can to make someone more comfortable, rather than do the most. And do know basically what to do.

Survival first aid outdoors

Apart from hypothermia, there are priorities among injuries which immediately endanger life and which are obvious. They have to be dealt with at once whether it is stoppage of breath or excessive bleeding.

Stay calm. Work according to a plan. And ask yourself if the patient now looks and/or feels more comfortable. If so, you have probably taken the correct action.

Again—

DON'T TOUCH THE PATIENT AT
  FIRST.

TAKE A CLOSER LOOK.

KEEP CALM.

STICK TO THE VERY SIMPLEST ES-
  SENTIALS OF FIRST AID.

Check the situation after an accident. Can you see how it happened? Dragging a friend onto a flat piece of grass who has just broken his back after falling down a mountainside will injure him even further and cause suffering.

Have a good look around the casualty. Keep the thought running through your mind to *only do what LITTLE you can to help.*

Somebody who has just been seriously hurt senses quickly enough if you panic and this will make him worse than ever. Never show you are scared but reassure and help the unfortunate person to ward off the effects of fear and shock which can kill just as much as the actual injuries. Look unmoved.

The following first-aid methods are listed in order of importance. An accident victim not breathing, or bleeding from an artery, obviously needs immediate treatment. Shock is a priority too—present to some degree in every person who meets with injury outdoors.

Kiss of life experiment

Drowning, asphyxiation (say, your tent was full of carbon monoxide fumes), and electrocution all mean absence of breathing. Go through the motions of the Kiss of Life so you know them by heart—it is not necessary actually to kiss the other person, but this does raise an important point. The fact you may have to kiss a stranger in an actual emergency will naturally inhibit any potential lifesaver. Likewise, many people fail to carry out the Kiss of Life in a real emergency because it seems so gruesome. There is a way to overcome this, however—place a handkerchief or piece of clothing over the victim's mouth and breathe through this.

Settle the casualty on his back.

Clear away any fluid, vomit, or foreign matter from the mouth with the forefinger (covered with a piece of cloth preferably).

Do this quickly.

Pull the head backward so the chin sticks upward toward the sky. Then drag the lower jaw forward to keep the tongue out of the air passage.

Hold the head quite still.

Make a final check that the casualty is not wearing false teeth (even your friend who is twelve years old might be wearing dentures). Remove them.

Open your mouth wide and—in a real emergency—clamp it firmly over the victim's opened mouth. You should also hold the casualty's nose between thumb and finger.

Blow into the open mouth (through a piece of cloth if necessary) into the lungs. Be gentle, especially if the person is a child—you could damage the lungs. But do blow quite firmly nevertheless.

Remove your mouth, and turn your head away. Listen for the rush of the air returning. And keep checking this way throughout your giving the Kiss of Life to a victim.

Continue blowing. The blowing rates differ according to size and age. For an adult or teen-ager, blow at the rate of twelve breaths a minute, counting five between each blow. For a small child, however, blow slow puffs at the rate of twenty a minute, counting three between breaths. It also helps to push on the child's stomach gently to remove any air here.

If there is no sign of any air exchange after a few minutes, inspect the position of the head again. Turn the patient on his side and slap between the shoulder blades to knock any stoppage loose.

Keep on breathing via the Kiss of Life until the person breathes on his own.

BLEEDING EXPERIMENT

The next time you cut a finger, imagine that it is not the relatively unimportant cut it is, but a deep gash that is gushing blood from an artery. First of all, let it bleed and note how a little blood looks a lot more than it really is. Now press the cut directly with the fingers to stop the bleeding. You would do the same with a serious wound. As long as you keep up the pressure, the flow of blood will slow and clot. It also helps—unless you suspect a broken bone—to raise a bleeding limb (then the blood is flowing uphill rather than downward). A pad (such as a clean handkerchief) is better. Keep this on the cut. Do not take it off when saturated (as it would be with an arterial gash), but add another cloth—any will do—on top. And so on, adding layers of material. Keep these dressings on after the blood has clotted. (It could take twenty minutes.)

Ordinary bleeding—as you are experiencing with your cut finger now—is best washed and left alone. Any piece of fairly clean cloth can be used as a dressing. This could be made more sterile by boiling in a covered container, or charring it.

Holding a chunk of ice to the cut will also stop the bleeding and help prevent infection. Germs cannot spread in the freezing cold.

Any INTERNAL BLEEDING could be dangerous. It will be caused by an accident—like a fall. Watch for blood coughed up or vomited, or traces of blood in the bowels. Do not give the person anything to drink, move him as little as possible, and go for help.

Bleeding from an ear could also be dangerous, and may follow an accident to the head. You need a doctor quickly.

Nose bleeding experiment

If your nose bleeds, tilt the head slightly forward and nip the nose just beneath the hard part for five minutes. The bleeding does not stop? Try again by blowing your nose to clear the bleeding side. Then nip the nose again. Do not clear the nose of clotted blood when the bleeding has stopped. A chunk of ice held over the bridge of the nose can also help in checking the bleeding. Don't remove the blood clot for several hours—you will get used to it.

CHOKING

This is a terrifying experience for the person concerned. Most of us have experienced the moment of panic when food has stuck in the gullet and we cannot breathe. We usually manage to cough it out or swallow it, but the danger is real—and grave. If this sounds alarming, it's precisely as it should be because only now are experts beginning to realize how common a killer choking is. (In America it is estimated that four thousand people each year die because food goes down the wrong way.) Emergency treatments vary.

The Heimlich Maneuver, named after a doctor at the Cincinnati Jewish Hospital, is favored by many authorities. It involves a bear hug from behind, with both hands joined firmly over the victim's diaphragm. The lungs are compressed and the air pressure forces the obstruction up and out of the throat.

It is possible to save choking victims from death simply by grasping the object with the fingers and pulling it out. But make sure there is enough of the object to give you a firm fingerhold—otherwise you might make matters worse by pushing it farther down.

Another method which has been used successfully many times is to sit the victim upright and thump firmly in the solar plexus. A firm blow in the right place empties the lungs, forcing air up the windpipe to push out the obstruction. (Should the person be suffering from a heart attack, one hard blow will do no harm; some doctors use exactly the same method to jar the heart back into regular rhythm.)

Under no circumstances should you apply the kiss of life until the object is removed. It is like trying to pour water into a corked bottle.

Experts disagree over the effectiveness of a hard slap between the shoulder blades, although the technique is thought to help where vomiting has occurred if the victim is placed face down. But if you do decide to use this method, turn an adult victim onto side and use heel of hand to slap hard between shoulder blades over the spine; a child may be turned upside down over an arm and handed two or three sharp blows between the shoulder blades.

Act fast. There is little time. By the time you have called a doctor it may be too late because it only takes a few minutes to choke to death.

SHOCK

Where there is physical injury there is also shock. The injury will usually look worse, but it is shock which can kill by its own effect alone. For instance, someone might break a leg and be in pain. Now the fractured limb will not kill, but if the accident happened in extremely traumatic circumstances, then the sudden shock to the system could conceivably be fatal. Always look for the signs and symptoms of shock in any survival situation.

These are: beads of sweat on the forehead; being sick; feeling faint; shivering; craving for a drink; clammy skin; suddenly knowing the real meaning of the words "feeling weak as a kitten"; dull eyes that are usually bright; a weak and rapid pulse; gasping for air.

Never take chances. Find warmth and shelter for the casualty, and anticipate that the more serious the wound, the more likely it is that shock will develop. It helps for the patient— possibly YOU and on your own—to lie with head lower than the feet to increase the flow of blood to the head.

If you are ALONE . . . keep yourself as warm as possible and rest for at least twenty-four hours when there is no way of reaching help quickly.

WARMTH . . . REASSURANCE . . . COMFORT are
the best treatment

BURNS

Never try to dress bad burns. Cover the victim with a clean piece of cloth. Try to keep him warm. And get to the nearest hospital as fast as possible. Do not try to treat by rubbing on ointments, butter, or any other substance. Ice, however, can give comfort to a burn. It will relieve pain, lessen swelling, and eliminate blisters. It is ideal for small burns.

Hold such smaller burns under running cold water for several minutes. Wash the surrounding skin with soap and water (not the burn itself, which is already sterile). Cover lightly with a dry, clean dressing or piece of cloth.

FRACTURES

The worst thing you can do is to try and straighten out a limb which is broken, or which you think has a break. Instead, remember those four key rules mentioned earlier and do not touch anything if it sends a spasm of pain through the casualty. Your aim is to make him comfortable; the one good sign that what little first aid you are applying is being—for the moment at least—successful. When the injuries are obviously severe, leave the victim where he is unless he is in danger of rolling off a ledge and into space. Build a shelter of any handy materials available around him, and get help.

Of course, if there is an open wound at the break, cover it lightly with a clean dressing or piece of cloth used as a make-do bandage (although this should not touch the wound so as to possibly infect it). When the fracture is bleeding, check the flow by pressing carefully with your fingers. Make sure, though, you are not jabbing on any broken ends of bones which can cause the patient to suffer even more shock.

Treat for shock as you check the bleeding. The patient needs to be kept snug and warm, and although he could well ask for a drink, do not give him one. Stay with the patient and give plenty of reassurance. Look for any opportunities of signaling help if the chance arises that someone is passing by in the distance. And, meanwhile, do your best to make the patient begin to feel better with constant assurance.

In certain instances you can try to ease the pain. But, if your measures hurt the patient, forget them. It is in the interest of comfort, above all else, that you should even consider certain tactics, and it is only if these measures do make the injured person feel a little happier that you are on the right line.

For example, you can cradle a broken arm or wrist in a sling made from a scarf or shirt folded into a triangle. Just rolled-up paper can make a useful splinter, as long as you do not bind it too tightly to the broken part. Although broken fingers need a doctor, you can sometimes ease the pain with a small splint made from a twig or anything else that is rigid and which will serve as a support. As for a fractured collarbone—well, for a start, you can usually tell when the person cannot move an arm and there is a sharp pain in the same shoulder. It is the kind of breakage that happens when you stumble and fall and put out an arm to save yourself. To ease the pain, the arm can be lifted across the chest and the cuff of the sleeve pinned to the shirt.

Leg fractures can be very serious. If the patient has to be moved, then pad in between the legs with spare clothing, and bind one leg to the other firmly but gently with strips of cloth. The general sequence of bandaging is one strip of cloth or whatever around the thighs, the knees, and the ankles, *and* a bandage above and below the actual fracture (but never pressing on it).

HEAD INJURIES

Count these as really serious and as something which needs a doctor as quickly as possible. Do not give someone so injured anything to eat or drink, and watch out for the danger signs after someone has suffered a blow on the head: trickles of blood from the ears or nose; pale and clammy skin; vomiting and sleepiness.

When the casualty is unconscious, lie him on one side. His face should be toward the ground. It will help to pad his underside with spare clothing. And touch his eyeballs to check that he is not just in a deep sleep. Loosen any tight clothing and keep a close watch on his breathing. It goes without saying by now that you should also keep him warm.

Supposing the accident was caused by pebbles falling down a rock face. They have struck your friend who is bleeding from the head. Now remember that a little blood looks like a lot—as already stressed—so keep calm. Sit him down and carefully press on the wound until the blood slows down and congeals. Of course, if there are embedded foreign bodies, like rock splinters, you must not press on these. Even small head cuts can need stitches; you need a doctor quickly.

SUNBURN

Sunburn is a common complaint of outdoor buffs in hot weather. Protect the person from further exposure. Cover the sunburned area with ointment or a substitute made by boiling the bark of an oak, hemlock, or chestnut tree.

Do not touch a sunburned area. Apply the ointment and cover the burn with a dressing. Do not remove the bandage except for emergency reasons or because it is dirty. Give the patient large amounts of fluid, and keep the burned area undisturbed.

SPRAINS

Bandage and rest the sprained limb. Chunks of ice help reduce the swelling and ease the pain—especially around the ankle. Cold applications should be kept up for the first twenty-four hours after injury, then apply heat.

A sprained limb *can* be used in a real emergency to the limit that the pain will allow; splint the injured area as effectively as possible.

CARRY SOMEBODY TO SAFETY

You can experiment with any of the simple carry-out methods shown in this diagram. Practice them all at home with friends.

Fireman's lift

Three-handed lift

Four- and two-handed lifts

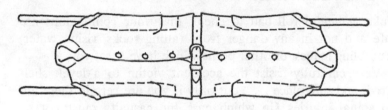

Makeshift stretcher

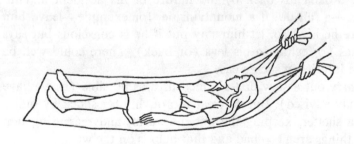

Drag sheet

WARNING: On no account lift anybody to
another place in a real crisis if you suspect

they could have a spinal injury. This can be established by gently feeling for tender spots and checking for paralysis or loss of feeling in the legs or back before moving the victim.

WHEN SOMEONE IN YOUR PARTY IS HURT

Know the correct procedure to take, and help all you can. It is common sense really, but things become confused and unimportant issues are sometimes dealt with first in the heat of the moment. Stick to priorities all the time, however, and you should be able to save the casualty a lot of injury—and possibly his life too—without risking your own.

Follow this procedure:

Take a mental roll call to check that your companions are safe and not in any danger from falling rocks, rising water, crumbling ledges, or other perils which have beset you.

Very carefully assist the accident victim to a level, sheltered, and safe place . . . but only if you are certain there are no spinal injuries (in which case the casualty must not be moved). If the person is unconscious, and you feel he may have broken his back by the nature of his accident and injuries—a fall down a mountainside, for example—leave him where he is. Also, let him stay put if he is conscious but says he has no feeling in his legs (or back). There could well be spine injuries in such a case.

Carry out as few first-aid measures as possible (as we have already advised). But do treat thoroughly for shock by building a shelter, keeping the patient warm, and reassuring him that things aren't so bad and that help is on the way.

And when you do have to send for help do it in this all-important sequence:

1. Always send two messengers if at all possible as they are much safer than one person alone. One runner is

vulnerable to any accident or misfortune that can happen along the way, and then, not only could he come to grief, but the original casualty is almost certainly in graver danger, too.

2. Send a written message. This should give location of the victim, the type of injuries, the time of the accident, and the number of people in the group.

3. Make sure the runners know the score. They must keep together and head quickly for the nearest main road, habitation, or telephone. "Quickly" is the key word; it doesn't mean "rush." Caution must not be sacrificed for the sake of speed, but don't waste time.

4. The runners should wait by the telephone for instruction from the rescue party (or police). Their job is not over. They need to guide the rescuers back to the victim.

Meanwhile, back at the casualty site, the people remaining should have everything under control: a tent pitched or a windbreak built; hot drinks brewed; spare clothing allocated between the patient and helpers (so the remaining helpers don't become chilled either); a fire burning; and SOS signals in readiness if help should appear over the horizon.

If there are only two of you

Imagine that the other person is injured and unconscious. You will have to stay with him and concentrate on signaling help as well as looking after the patient. Another special task is to build a good shelter.

If, however, the other person is conscious, go for help after leaving a flag, large pile of rocks, or other marker. Leave equipment with the injured person which will help—a sleeping bag and gas stove, for example.

In case it is decided a helicopter rescue is imperative, lay out large symbols that can be seen from the air as in chapter

7. They should be 8 ft. (2 m.) in height, or larger when possible, and made from fabric, wood, stones, or stamping in the snow.

Helping the rescuers

Mark your route on the way out to reach help. Then when you find it, you can lead a rescue party back to the survival scene without hesitation. Rock piles, knife slashes on trees, marks trampled in the snow . . . all help en route.

Advise the rescue party of the information listed on your piece of paper before you set off (as above), the distance of the casualty off the beaten track (or any nearby path or road), the kind of terrain, how long it will probably take to reach the victim, what equipment and how many helpers are probably needed. Of course, they will probably know much of your information, and the matter will be taken out of your hands. But every little scrap of information helps at this stage.

Now, here are two instances of the type of rescue in which you may find yourself involved—stories of which can make national newspaper headlines.

Help a helicopter pilot

Helicopters are being used more and more for rescue when life is at stake in the Great Outdoors. If YOU are the victim in a remote area as the helicopter homes in on you—and there is nobody else to help—assist the pilot all you can.

For a start, do not continue flashing your signaling mirror when it is obvious the helicopter pilot has seen you; you can blind, distract, or just plain irritate him.

Helicopter landing road test

Practice the ways, in a park or nearby field, in which a group of people on the ground can aid a helicopter pilot.

Choose a flat landing zone (LZ) about twenty yards

square. Remove rocks, branches, bracken, molehills, or whatever. Fill in ruts, holes, and ditches. Now peg a bright-colored marker in the center of the LZ. (Any bright square of cloth will do.)

It will assist the pilot if you show which way the wind is blowing. You are unlikely to have a smoke cartridge handy, but you can often build a fire in time (especially if you had prepared for emergency signaling as described in chapter 7). The smoke should blow on the pilot's right-hand side as he approaches the LZ upwind.

No smoke? Stand with your back to the wind instead. Flash a flashlight into the wind—away from the oncoming helicopter. And know the best rescue spot: on the right-hand side of the approach path. Check that you are well clear of the LZ—and the lethal helicopter blades.

Approach the helicopter from 45°—in front. The safest side to be on is the pilot's—you can see him, and he, you. Do not go near the tail of the machine—the rotor can chop you clean in two.

Certain rescue sites are too dangerous for helicopters—like ledges on cliff faces. Do not worry about this if you are marooned in such a situation. It will be taken out of your hands . . . whether the pilot and winchman decide to use the *single lift, the double lift* (where the victim is helped by the winchman), or the *stretcher lift*.

This type of rescue is seen best when you are in peril at sea. To rescue people from a boat, the helicopter lowers a member of the crew on a cable. He then aids the victims by fitting them—one by one—into a harness which is then winched up to the helicopter with the crew man accompanying the casualty.

Follow these tips if such a situation ever has you as one of its star participants:

1. Stow away all sails in a small boat, at the approach of the helicopter. The downdraft of its main rotor is

incredibly gusty; it can knock a small boat flat if sails are still set.

2. A helicopter may not be able to lift casualties straight from the doomed boat as there may be too many obstructions on board. Be ready, therefore, for an inflatable dinghy being lowered, or launch a rubber dinghy or life raft on instructions.

3. Be ready for an electric shock when you touch the winch cable, caused by the static charge due to the helicopter's friction with the air. Forget any eagerness and wait until the cable, and whatever attachments it has for carrying you—sling, basket, or even a forest penetrator (designed to make its way down through a canopy of tree foliage)—has touched the ground or water and consequently leaked its charge of static electricity.

4. Take off boots, but NOT socks, if you have to go into the water.

5. Go limp when lifted by the winch. The helicopter's crew will find it so much easier if you prove a dead weight rather than a live one.

ASSIST A BEACHGUARD

As surf crashes on the shore, you may be requested to help in a rescue out among the frothing tide. A lifeguard going to the aid of someone drowning in the surf, and wearing a safety belt, may need somebody to handle the attached line and reel. He will brief you, but know the drill in advance.

It is easy to do as long as you are not too zealous. As in survival first aid, it pays to do as little as possible, *but to do it carefully.*

But do these things:

Do watch the lifeguard wearing the nonbuoyant safety belt.

Do pull in when he raises an arm. (He will have demonstrated exactly when he wishes you to pull.)

Do not pull in too quickly. (This could submerge victim and the beltman.)

INDEX

Accidents (*see also* specific aspects, kinds, *e.g.*, Automobiles; Bleeding; Boats; Caves; Choking; Climbing; Livesaving; Lost; Snow): calling for help, 110–33, 192–93 (*see also* Calling for Help); first aid, 180–97 (*see also* First aid); helping rescuers, 194–97; locating site (direction finding), 164–70

Airplane and helicopter pilots, calling for help from, 113–15, 119, 193–94 (*see also* Helicopter rescues); SOS writing in sand or snow, 129–30

Animal food, hunting and cooking, 148–51, 153, 155

Animal life, threats from, 91–95; bee or wasp stings, 92; dogs, 93–94; horses and cows, 94; snakes, 93; swans, 95

Arm or wrist fractures, 188

Arrow ground-to-air signals, 114, 115

A-shaped plastic-sheet tents, 30

Asphyxiation: carbon monoxide, 72–73, 182–83; choking and, 185–86; Heimlich Maneuver, 185; Kiss of Life (breathing) method, 182

Attacks (assaults), 8–11; animals, 91–95; intruders, 20–21; kicks, 10–11; running from weapons, 11; strong-arm tips, 8–11

Automobiles (accidents, emergencies), 6–13 (*see also* Accidents; First aid); assaults (*see* Attacks); braking, 12, 13; hitchhiking and, 7–8; money safety, 6–7; signaling for help, 112 (*see also* Signals); skidding, 13; snowbound, 66–67; tricky driving, 11–13; water on road, 11–13

Avalanches, 87–88

Backpackers, distress signals and, 115–17

Bandaging fractures, 188

Barn shelters, 63–64

Basement, snow, 59–60

Bat wings, 89–90

Beds and bedding material, outdoor, 58–59, 66, 137

Bee stings, 92; extracting, 92

Bicycles, 11–13; braking, 12, 13; tricky driving, 11–13; wet roads, 11–13

Birch bark, as fuel, 34, 38

Birds: cooking, 156; eggs, 143, 153

Birthday cake candle, 43; "magic," 43

Bites: bees or wasps, 92; dogs, 93–94; snakes, 93

Bivouac sites, selecting, 135–37

Bivvy bags, 26–28

Bleeding, first aid and, 181, 182, 183–84; dressings, 184; ear, 184;

Anthony Greenbank, who has been a full-time writer since 1960, was formerly an Outward Bound instructor. He has become widely known as an authority on survival and has published several highly successful books on the subject in Britain and America, including *The Book of Survival* and *Survival in the City*. Mr. Greenbank lives in the English Lake District where he pursues his avocations of rock-climbing and mountaineering.